ALSO BY PAGE DICKEY

Gardens in the Spirit of Place

Dogs in Their Gardens

Cats in Their Gardens

Breaking Ground

Inside Out: Relating Garden to House

Duck Hill Journal

D0971152

EMBROIDERED GROUND

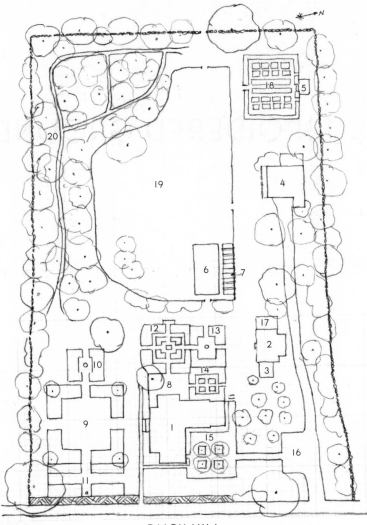

DUCK HILL

Garden Plan

1. House
2. Boscotel
3. Greenhouse
4. Barn
5. Chicken house
6. Pool
7. Arbor
8. Kitchen terrace
9. Main garden
10. White garden
11. Hemlock garden
12. Herb garden
13. Yellow garden
14. Nasturtium garden
15. Courtyard
16. Parking
17. Boscotel terrace
18. Vegetable garden
19. Meadow
20. Woodland

EMBROIDERED GROUND

REVISITING THE GARDEN

PAGE DICKEY

ILLUSTRATIONS BY WILLIAM ATHERTON

FARRAR, STRAUS AND GIROUX   NEW YORK

Farrar, Straus and Giroux
18 West 18th Street, New York 10011

Distributed in Canada by D&M Publishers, Inc.
Printed in the United States of America
First edition, 2011

Library of Congress Cataloging-in-Publication Data
Dickey, Page.
    Embroidered ground : revisiting the garden / Page Dickey. — 1st ed.
        p. cm.
    ISBN 978-0-374-25632-6 (alk. paper)
    1. Gardening—New York (State)—North Salem. 2. Duck Hill Garden
(North Salem, N.Y.). 3. Dickey, Page—Homes and haunts—New York
(State)—North Salem. I. Title.

SB453.2.N7D54 2010
635.909747'277—dc22

                                                            2010015543

Designed by Jonathan D. Lippincott

www.fsgbooks.com

1 3 5 7 9 10 8 6 4 2

FOR MELISSA

Gardening, reading about gardening,
and writing about gardening are all one;
no one can garden alone.
                    —Elizabeth Lawrence

CONTENTS

CONTENTS

CONTENTS

ILLUSTRATIONS

PREFACE

My youngest daughter, Jean, was teased in college for living in a house with its own name. But I was half laughing when I called our new home Duck Hill thirty years ago. We had moved from a place substantial in architecture and history to this plain yellow and white box, built of clapboard and field-stone, perched on the side of a hill, and it reminded me of a duck standing there in its simple, slightly forlorn charm. Why did I feel I had to name the place at all? Because I was keeping a diary, and knew I would write about it, and wanted to call it something.

Nine years later, I wrote a book, *Duck Hill Journal*, about the garden I was making here, how I wanted it to be in keep-ing with the farmhouse, equally prim in its hedged outlines, just as unpretentious, with perennials and shrubs that might have been here when it was built in the nineteenth century—a garden fragrant and homely, with an old-fashioned air and charm. Now, standing back and looking at the garden two de-cades later, I realize I took grand ideas—long axes, straight vistas, tall enclosing hedges, repeated sentinels of boxwood—and half laughed at them too, simplified them, brought down their scale to suit the house, made them intimate rather than imposing.

The garden has burgeoned since I first plotted its outlines, has filled out, matured, its structure satisfyingly substantial, the trees grown, the hedges high. It is blowsy now, not as fresh-faced, its edges no longer crisp, its ground crowded to bursting with the inevitable collection of too many plants over the years. Suddenly, in a middle-aged garden, we reach a point when we have to take stock, stand back, think about renewal, renovation, hacking back, shrinking, adapting. And in tackling this renewal, our enthusiasm and energy are rekindled. For it is the *process* of making—or remaking—a garden that engages and thrills us.

At barely three acres, Duck Hill's garden is not large by country standards, though more than we can easily maintain, surrounded by high open fields on the east, south, and west and a strip of young scrappy woods on the north. We see neighboring houses, many more than when I first settled here in North Salem, but an aura of pastoral serenity still permeates this town merely sixty miles from New York City, on the edge of New England. The road we live on is dirt, not asphalt. The crowing of our roosters is echoed by others in neighboring yards, cows are still heard lowing from open hills across the valley, riders on horseback clop down our street.

These are lingering sentiments, vestiges of the bustling farm community that was here in the mid-nineteenth century, when our house was built. Dairy cows then littered our rolling pastureland, apple orchards ordered the high rocky ground, and cider and grain mills lined the Titicus River, which cuts through our valley. Now those mills are charming houses, and the pastures are more apt to harbor fancy horses than milk cows. The mooing I hear when I'm gardening is from a small herd of beef cattle that are someone's hobby. Old gnarled apple trees are spotted all over town in backyard gardens, or standing incongruously in woodland, or rotting in once-active commercial orchards now choked with poison ivy and bittersweet.

The garden at Duck Hill was young and crisp-edged when I first wrote about it, and I was young then too, with boundless energy and dreams, driven by passion and a desire to experiment and learn as I dug ever more ground to cultivate, to plant. As the garden grew and changed, my life changed also, with my children grown and gone, with divorce, years of travel, remarriage. The passion remains, the deep pleasure in the garden, though I have a fraction of the vigor I once had, with bones that now creak and muscles that scream in protest. My thoughts on gardening have changed too, colored by my own experience, my successes and failures, and by what I've learned in traveling, visiting other gardens, and writing of other gardeners' visions and artistry.

"How lucky you are, meeting gardeners and seeing gardens all over the country and around the world," people say to me. And I always answer yes, I consider myself fortunate. My passion and my work are one and the same. The many gardens I've seen have deeply influenced my own vision, my own aesthetic. And the friends I've made among the gardeners I've met are some of my dearest. But I feel most lucky to be able to return to my patch of earth, to add stitches to its woven tapestry, to use the knowledge I've gained, to feed the passion. In reflection, and with an eye to the future, I wanted to write about it again.

A STROLL THROUGH
DUCK HILL

THE FLOWER GARDENS

No gardens were here, no flowers at all other than some twisted, shaggy-barked stands of lilacs that bloomed lavishly in May. When I came to Duck Hill thirty years ago, I was faced with a featureless canvas, nothing but ragged lawn and rough grass surrounding the house, and a young, weed-choked wood and a small field beyond. I brought with me a few treasures from my previous home—a clump of lungwort, *Pulmonaria angustifolia*, gentian blue in April, carried from home to home since it was given to me by generous neighbors when I was twenty-three and gardening with babies at my feet; a division of a May-blooming, fragrant daylily, golden yellow and star-shaped with brown dashes on the backs of its petals, related, I suspect, to the species *Hemerocallis dumortieri*. It was originally a gift from a friend named John and ever after has been called "John's day-lily." I brought snowdrops, winter aconites, and Dutchman's breeches from the woods I used to own, a few tubers of a delicate white Siberian iris that naturalized in the meadow there, and several young bushes of antique roses—albas, damasks, gallicas—that I couldn't bear to leave behind. These, and more, I heeled into a square of dirt in the field above the house where the previous owners had had a vegetable patch. Then I plotted my first garden.

The old farmhouse sat squat and prim, facing south, in an open, sun-filled spot above a river valley. The maple that once stood by its front door had long since died, but ancient sugar maples and white ash still surrounded the property at its perimeters, providing shade at a distance and a beautiful backdrop. That first autumn, I staked out and dug flower beds around a fifty-foot-square piece of lawn just below the house, using the front door as the central axis. I ignored the fact that the land sloped a bit away from the house to the south, for, with limited means, I couldn't afford terracing, and I knew at least that the flowers would like the good drainage and exposure. The angled beds were generous in size, a good ten feet deep (and became more generous over the years, as straightening the edges each spring meant cutting away a little more lawn). I enriched the soil with manure from a neighboring farm and compost I had brought from my old garden, let the beds settle over winter, and in the spring planted them with the treasures I had heeled into the field. Other perennials, grown from seed or bought from mail-order nurseries, were added, and in the fall, daffodils, tulips, alliums, and Asiatic lilies were woven into the mix. To frame and enclose the garden, I planted a hedge around its outer edges.

Today, the main garden—for that is what we call it, because of its ample size and seniority—remains essentially the same, though inevitably some of its inhabitants have changed over the years. Shrub roses—gallicas, rugosas, *Rosa moyesii*, *R. glauca*—still share the beds with sturdy perennials, grasses, and bulbs, in a color scheme that is dictated by the roses' bluish pinks and velvety plums, combined with hues of blue, white, and clear yellow. In each of the four corners, a crab apple tree (the variety 'Katherine') offers some shade. It is a small-growing crab, slightly pendulous in habit with foliage that, I've discovered, doesn't flourish in our humid summers, becoming powdered with mildew and curling in distaste; but it is a memorable pink and white confection for a week in May. Great boxwood bushes mark the four entrances into the garden, axes of a central cross that cut through the enclosing privet hedge, which is now six feet high and clipped to a sharp horizontal line.

Because this garden is large in scale and seen across a generous square of lawn, bold stands and sweeps of plants seem to work best. Each month has its show, starting in April with the beloved lungwort, which paints the ground blue beneath the crabs and threads through later-blooming perennials in the back of the borders. In May the brief but glamorous flowering of the peonies is accompanied by amsonia's sky blue haze of starry flowers, and finally the early roses, the double pinks and deep crimsons of rugosas, tall silver-and-plum-leaved *R. glauca* with its tiny pink and white flowers, and *R. moyesii*, equally tall and arching, its branches studded with simple flowers of deepest red. Groves of lace-white sweet cicely (*Myrrhis odorata*) and fern-leaf tansy, hostas, iris, heucheras, and burnets offer a counterpoint of richly patterned foliage. By July the garden is brightened by clear yellow daylilies, pink burnets, and coneflowers. Joe-Pye weed is allowed to bully its way into the back of the borders, and its great umbels of soft mauvy pink in August and September complement speciosum lilies and wheels of summer phlox in rose pink and white. Asters bring a haze of blue and purple to the borders in autumn, and the waving seed heads of grasses here—pennisetum, deschampsia, panicum, hakonechloa—are at their most beautiful.

To set off the bold plantings in the main garden, the stretch of lawn serves as a quiet plane, a negative space, so rare and precious in a gardener's garden. We forget in our insane desire to have ever-more plants how important it is to have *unplanted* stretches as contrast, simple planes—lawn, field, sky. Fifteen years ago, in my madness, I considered cutting up that square of lawn to add four large, square flower beds (oh, the sun! the roses I could grow!) so that this garden would be nothing but beds intersected by grass paths. In a dreamy way, I plotted it out on graph paper. But my oldest daughter, Kim, hearing of my scheme, pleaded with me not to, saying she hoped one day to be married on that piece of lawn. Who would not listen to such a plea? And indeed she was married there, on a sunlit June evening in 2001. We woke to rain that day, buckets of it, and in the afternoon I caught a trickle of tears on Kim's face as we walked in our slickers and boots up to the tent in our back field where we knew the wedding ceremony would have to be. But just as the guests were arriving, the rain stopped and the clouds gave way to golden end-of-the-afternoon sun. We hurriedly wiped off the chairs, set them on the lawn, and rolled out a red carpet, and she had her garden wedding. The year before, on another beautiful evening, Bosco and I had celebrated our own marriage on the same patch of grass.

The cross path in the main garden leads to smaller gardens on each side. To the west, in a half-shaded spot, I made a small enclosure of white flowers, finding the idea of such a limited palette appealing. Its luminous blooms, I knew, would light up this shadowy place, and shimmer with the approach of nightfall. Its diminutive size, thirty-five feet by forty, was not at all intended, but dictated by the discovery of a septic tank on one side and septic fields on the other. Unexpected developments such as these often give a garden character. The smallness of the white garden turned out to be its asset, giving it a sense of intimacy in contrast to the large, open feel of the main garden. Two bracket-shaped borders are backed by a three-foot-high boxwood hedge, which highlights the white flowers and the silver and variegated leaves. Four large, round bushes of box mark the little garden's central grass path, and a stone vase, sporting white violas in spring and variegated geraniums in summer, stands in the center. Much is made of bulbs in this garden—white-flowering daffodils, tulips, alliums, and lilies—

for they take little room and generally pack a punch. Single-flowered white peonies, *Campanula latiloba* 'Alba', summer phlox, and lacy-leaved burnets with bottlebrush blooms weave through the beds. White Japanese anemones and false asters, *Boltonia asteroides*, offer a final show. Despite the tiny size of this space, I included several shrubs for weight and winter interest—two fragrant white rugosa roses, the elegant *Rosa* × *dupontii*, hydrangeas, a variegated dogwood. Just as overscale furniture is sometimes effective in a small room, statuesque plants can often be charming if unexpected in a small garden.

For many years, an old white ash shaded this little place, and, under its limbs, I clustered chairs for lingering with a glass of ice tea or wine. The ash is gone, felled by the fungus that is sweeping this area, and has been replaced by a young hybrid dogwood; but the chairs are still here. Sitting here many years ago, I was struck by the fact that, at the opposite end of the axis through the white garden and the main garden, I was look-ing at a blank green wall, namely, the tall hemlock hedge that screened our property from the road. I felt something needed to be added to end the perspective and catch your eye: a statue, perhaps, or a large, beautiful vase. As a temporary measure, I placed an old stone urn we had in front of the hedge, a little too fancy in style, I thought, but all right until I found some-thing more appropriate. The urn is still there.

The space between the main garden's privet hedge and the hemlock hedge was long and narrow, quiet and green, a grass walk barely twenty feet wide and sixty feet long. What fine back-drops those hedges would make for a double border of flow-ers, I thought one day, and proceeded impetuously to dig beds all along their lengths. I scattered hybrid rugosa roses down the long borders, and underplanted them with perennials and bulbs (in like colors of clear pink, magenta, plum, and cream) that would offer a succession of flowering and good foliage from spring through fall. I dotted boxwood bushes down the edges of the beds, for contrast as well as added structure and winter color. The hemlock garden became a pretty place for a number of years, romantic and heady with fragrance when the roses were blooming, and pleasing in its limited color scheme. Cranesbills in various pinks and magenta carpeted the ground in summer, and plum-colored burnets, spotted foxgloves, and pink astilbes added vertical plumes and spires; in autumn, low asters washed the beds with pink and white, and the charming bush clover, *Lespedeza thunbergii*, exploded with a fountain of magenta pea flowers.

Having three garden rooms of soft and muted colors, I longed for something fiery—yellow, red, orange, gold. Just beyond the kitchen terrace to the north, there was a scruffy grass slope that burned out with the first hint of a drought, remaining an eyesore through much of the summer. With the help of a stonemason, the slope was terraced with small retaining walls and steps, and in beds between gravel paths I planted what I called the nasturtium garden. Visitors are always asking where the nasturtiums are, but I named the garden that not because it contains nasturtiums particularly (we do plug some in occasionally), but because it celebrates those luscious hot colors. Daylilies are the stars here from May through October, mostly species and early hybrids that are fragrant and star-shaped in golden yellows, oranges, and rusty reds. Poppies are here in abundance, the old-fashioned orangey red oriental packed with crepe paper crinolines, and a fragile paler Atlas poppy that flowers through much of the summer. A winterberry, *Ilex verticillata* 'Winter Gold', with berries that are not gold but a luminous orange, and a black pussy willow (*Salix melanostachys*) serve as a backdrop to this garden, and six box bushes mark its central path. In summer we add tender cupheas and crocosmia in pots for some extra shots of scarlet and orange.

Yellow has seeped into another small garden on the other side of the pussy willow, an extension of the herb garden that unfolds its pattern above the kitchen terrace. This was originally my vegetable garden, and laughable as such, with barely enough room among annual flowers for a few rows of lettuces, one maybe of beans, and a tomato plant or two. The vegetable garden finally graduated to a respectable size at the back of the property behind the barn. Now this is the last of the flower gardens we pass through on the way to the barn or the meadow and pool, a small graveled enclosure surrounded by beds of clear yellow, white, and blue flowers with a sporadic dash of red. A fence fashioned from locust posts and thin locust branches borders this garden, half obscured by the shrub rose 'Harrison's Yellow', an old twisting-branched purple-leaved smokebush, *Viburnum plicatum* 'Summer Snowflake', and the black salix. Perennial yellow daisies—the tall willowy *Helianthus* 'Lemon Queen' and coreopsis (our native *C. tripteris*)—along with a white selection of Joe-Pye weed, its great heads alive with butterflies, back the garden with blooms in summer. Miniature trumpet daffodils and the pale sky blue grape hyacinth 'Valerie Finis' bring the borders alive in early spring. A stone rooster on a round pedestal marks the center of this small garden and is surrounded first by pots of yellow violas and later, in summer, by agapanthus and pineapple lilies (varieties of eucomis).

These rooms of flowers, each with a character and color scheme of its own, were added gradually over the years, not with any master plan in mind, but one by one, as the desire took me, but always connected with a strong axis in the form of a path, so that you catch glimpses of one garden from another, and are lured on in your stroll around the house.

THE HERB GARDEN

Just beyond the kitchen, on a piece of slanting ground that was leveled by the previous owners to accommodate a plastic aboveground pool, I hacked away at the stony earth that first year to make a garden of herbs. I planned the garden in a geometric pattern of small beds and gravel paths around a central sundial, using the kitchen door as my main axis. An opposite axial path led down a few steps to the eventual white garden on the south, and up a step to what is now the little yellow garden to the north. Boxwood bushes were planted to mark the entrances and a hedge, originally of barberry I regret to say, was planted around its perimeter. Because the garden was raised—up several stone steps from the kitchen terrace—it was high and dry and sunny, just what most herbs crave.

It is a garden primarily of scents, pungent and sweet, some thrown into the air, others released as we rub a leaf or tread on a green carpet, a medley of perfumes on a summer's day from thymes, sages, artemisias, lavenders, and mints; tansy and sweet cicely; pinks and roses. It is a garden for touching and smelling, for snipping: a garden of lore and history too, for there are endless tales of how these plants were used over the centuries, and still are, in medicine, as dyes or bug repellents, in cooking and the making of perfume.

The garden is prettiest in June, when the thymes that spill out of the beds are studded with tiny mauve and white flow-

The herb garden

ers, and blue-green mats of cheddar pinks and cottage pinks are littered with spicy pinwheels, and the roses, ancient damasks and gallicas prized for their perfume, are daily opening their sweet muddled blooms. *Rosa mundi*, streaked and splashed with crimson, pink, and white, fills one corner, its branches low and spreading to four feet, through which starry, spherical heads of *Allium christophii* thrust and explode. Spears of Florentine iris in ghostly gray-white flower accompany the rose 'Leda', sometimes called the painted damask, extravagantly dressed in white petals tipped in crimson, a graceful five-foot shrub that weeps over the hedge near the kitchen terrace. Pink ruffled 'Celsiana', another gorgeously fragrant damask, mingles with furry apple mint, sweet cicely, and bee balm (*Monarda didyma*) in another corner. Bushes of the gas plant, *Dictamnus albus*, in white and streaky mauve add their lemony scent and are valued verticals along with foxgloves and, later, tall yellow and white mulleins, varieties of verbascum.

A few of the herbs I thought essential to the garden's design were eventually abandoned when their unsuitability to our climate became painfully obvious. Santolina, also known as lavender cotton, is the herb I miss most, for, in its pale gray-green form, it was the young garden's most telling feature. This Mediterranean plant has odd coral-like leaves and a round, clumping habit that, along with its silvery color, makes it a strikingly effective border plant. I planted it by the dozen, in ribbons around the four central beds, loving the way it contrasted with the rich and varied greens of other herbs. But santolina does not like our hot, humid summers, let alone our fierce winters. It began to die in droves. I stubbornly replaced the felled plants with new versions, even went to the extreme of digging out and replacing the soil when I realized a fungus lurking there was doing them in. But the plants continued to die, without warning, overnight, invariably in the middle of the summer when it was really too hot to be replanting, and I finally gave up. Culinary sage and curly chives, *Allium senescens glaucum*, were planted in their stead, not as striking as the lavender cotton, but infinitely happier here, staying attractive throughout summer and fall.

Germander, the handsome low-growing *Teucrium fruticans*, is another herb I used extensively at first but no longer rely on. I planted it as a front edging, enjoying its deep green, crimped foliage, compact habit, and magenta spikes in late summer. But it was always slow to come to life in spring, still brown twigs and seemingly dead for much of May—and in some years after harsh winters, it didn't bother to leaf out at all. I don't grow nearly as much lavender as I did at first, for it too does not thrive in our climate. With the years, we learn to settle for the plants that like our situation, that flourish despite the wildly fluctuating cold of winter freezing and spells of extended mugginess in summer.

I depend a great deal on the different sages in this garden, especially the varieties of cooking sage (*Salvia officinalis*) with silver, golden-variegated, or purple-tinted leaves, for they are handsome all summer and effective planted in sweeps along the front edges of the beds. Sometimes the golden sort does not survive our wet winters, but then I treat it as an annual and plant it again in the spring. I find it that essential. Other truly tender sages are added yearly for their racemes of late summer color—the scarlet pineapple sage (with leaves that really do smell of pineapple), deep blue *S. guaranitica* hybrids, sky blue *S. uliginosa*, the velvety lavender and white 'Phyllis Fancy'. These flowering sages as well as red bee balm will guarantee daily visits of hummingbirds.

Southernwood, *Artemisia abrotanum*, is a stalwart favorite, not for its flowering, which is inconsequential, but for its feathery foliage, which adds a soft haze to the garden beds. The same plants, only occasionally divided, have been in the garden here from its beginning. I cut them back hard in April (this is done to all the woody herbs—lavender, thyme, rue, sage) and then give them a light clipping in early August, each time enjoying their pungent, camphorlike odor. Sprigs of southernwood, called *garde-robe* in France, are still valued as a moth repellent. Nose-twisting rue is also considered a bug repellent, sometimes tucked into a horse's bridle to ward off flies. I like to mass bushes of rue in a bed, for its leaves, glaucous blue-green and scalloped, serve as an effective contrast to more linear or ferny foliage. Half the fun of a herb garden, I think, is playing with the richly varied colors and textures of its leaves. But isn't that half the fun of any sort of garden? Perhaps what makes an enclosure of herbs unique is the heady intensity of its interwoven fragrances.

The sundial at the center of our herb garden has been replaced with a round stone trough of water for the birds and dragonflies. The barberry, a notorious invader, has been succeeded by a fragrant lilac hedge. The garden is wilder than when I first made it, its denizens now barely controlled, but it remains the same in essence, a deeply sensual place to linger in or to stroll through on a warm summer day.

THE SMALL WOODLAND

If you step down from the herb garden and walk south past the magnolia on your right and the white garden on your left, you come to the beginning of the woodland. Hostas and ferns spread at its entrance among Virginia sweetspire, fothergillas, and oakleaf hydrangeas, and dogwoods mark the start of the path that leads you through this wild shadowy place, wending west then turning north, past a wooden bench at its far corner, toward the vegetable garden and the meadow in the sunlit distance.

I didn't go about making the woodland garden in a proper way, the way I knew any sort of garden should be made. I had no plan, other than knowing this tree-littered spit of land along the south boundary of our property would be my shade garden. Nor did I have the energy or time in those first years to tackle the poison ivy, brambles, barberry, bittersweet, garlic mustard, and celandine that flourished there. Nevertheless, the very first autumn after moving to Duck Hill, I planted bulbs—daffodils, snowdrops, aconites—in the middle of the mess, simply clearing and enriching small circles of ground around them. Each subsequent year, I haphazardly tucked in a few dozen more bulbs, as well as a primrose here or a hellebore there, with a shovelful of compost, ignoring the surrounding tangle. Every spring I divided clumps of snowdrops as their flowers faded, replanting them in ever-widening patches among the weeds, imagining, hoping for, a March picture of drifts of luminous white beneath the trees. In my impulsiveness, I made it impossible to ever prepare this garden properly.

Before planting those first bulbs, I should have marked paths and mapped out the areas I eventually wanted to plant beneath the trees, and then, section by section, grubbed out the woody weeds and smothered the herbaceous sorts with layers of newspaper covered with compost and left to decompose over the winter. I should have thought about the garden's composition: how I would have complementary waves of ground covers mingling with spring ephemerals beneath flowering woodland shrubs, how I would extend interest beyond spring with late-flowering and beautifully textured and patterned plants. But I did none of that. I was too busy making the flower gardens around the house and planting ornamental trees and shrubs there to give the woodland the attention it deserved.

It got that attention, finally, with Bosco's arrival eleven years ago. He brought a dowry of shade plants from his old garden in Irvington, New York—wonderfully cut and crinkled ferns and a large collection of epimediums, descendants of plants from the garden of the renowned plantsman Harold Epstein—and these needed a proper home. And so we high-pruned the existing trees to let in more light, cutting down any that were misshapen or crowded, then wove primary and secondary paths through them to create opportunities for intimate viewing of woodland treasures. We pulled and smothered the weeds, bit by bit (we are still at it), enriching each new area with leafy compost, working gingerly around plants already established. We added more shrubs and small trees, bringing interest and beauty to that important middle ground of a woodland understory—native azaleas, viburnums, clethra, witch hazels, oakleaf hydrangeas, shad, and dogwoods. Bosco's elegant epimediums now billow along the paths' edges in company with the hellebores we began to collect. They are intermingled with as many of the enchanting spring ephemerals as we can afford. Primroses proliferate as long as I remember to divide and replant them every two or three years and water them in dry summers. Violets of all colors, every species and hybrid that catches my eye, are allowed to romp. Ferns are added yearly.

In earliest spring, when the air is still chill and the garden beds around the house are damp and slow to wake, this patch of woodland is alive with small happenings that thrill us. The witch hazels are studded with yellow, and snowdrops flower beneath them and all along the paths, mostly the ordinary *Galanthus nivalis* in its single and double forms, their pearl whiteness, yes, drifts of it, shimmering on an overcast day or at dusk. We grow some of the rarer hybrids too, their differences appreciated only when you stoop to lift their teardrop outer petals and inspect their inner configuration and markings, sorts like 'Lady Elphinstone', whose demure white segments hide an inner perianth of white satin crinolines edged in yellow. Winter aconites, *Eranthis hyemalis*, appear almost as early as the snowdrops, needing only some gentle sun to open wide their waxy bright yellow cups that rest on ruffs of deeply cut greenery. Hellebores (the white Christmas rose, *Helleborus niger*, and the many cultivars of the Lenten rose, *H. orientalis*) open their white, pink, and deep burgundy cups by the beginning of March, in a mild winter even earlier. They are extraordinarily long-blooming, remaining in flower through all of spring. Like snowdrops, their blooms, upturned, reveal hidden beauty, jewel-like spotted interiors sometimes washed with sea green or slate or turquoise.

As early as weather permits, I cut away the hellebores' old tattered leaves, so that their flowers rest on nothing but fingers of fresh green. Seedlings crop up around the skirts of the Lenten roses, and these we move to roomier quarters after they've developed two or more leaves. The hellebores appreciate a slightly sweet soil, so if your soil is acid, some lime added at planting time is beneficial. The plantsman Dan Hinkley suggests using pieces of blackboard chalk inserted in the soil, and I now keep some in my pocket to plant with new hellebores.

A tiny purple violet blooms early in spring, along with the first of the primroses, the charming red-violet *Primula abshasica*, first given to me years ago by my colleague Sidney Eddison, who has a beguiling primrose path in her woodland in Connecticut. The coloring of this early primrose harmonizes with the mauve corydalis, *C. solida*, which crops up around it. New selections of this woodland corydalis now on the market are even more desirable, such as clear pink 'Beth Evans' and 'White Knight'. By April, hepaticas, possibly my favorites among the spring ephemerals, open their tiny, exquisitely dainty stars of sky blue or white above mottled and patterned heart-shaped leaves. The eight-petalled, cupped flowers of the twinleaf open fleetingly then too, our native white *Jeffersonia diphylla*, which generously multiplies in our woods, and the gorgeous blue Japanese *J. dubia*, which does not. The leaves of the jeffersonias, which develop into handsome clumps, are of even greater value, "two-parted affairs that look like sets of butterfly wings floating above the ground," as Bill Cullina describes them in his fine book on wildflowers. Bloodroots appear as suddenly, their furled white blooms at first clasped by scalloped leaves, pale gray-green on their backsides, the single, roselike flowers expanding for merely a day or two before shattering onto the ground. The double bloodroots, packed tightly with petals like small camellias, last longer in bloom, and increase into good patches with time.

By the beginning of May, all the anemones and rue anemones are flowering in white, clear yellow, blue—even pink—winsome blooms, double or single. I cannot imagine having too many of them, although, like so many of these fragile spring flowers, they will go dormant in the heat of summer and so need to be woven among burgeoning hellebores and heucheras, ferns and epimediums, primroses and violets—plants that will remain in leaf through summer and fall. By the middle of May, sheets of woodland phlox, *P. divaricata* and the shorter *P. stolonifera*, have transformed this shaded garden with a haze of soft, silvery lavender-blue from their whirls of flowers. Tiarellas are in bloom too, their fuzzy white and pink stalks a nice contrast to the phlox, and all sorts of trilliums are opening, the tall wine-purple *T. erectum*, the pale yellow *T. luteum*, the glistening white *T. grandiflorum*. Solomon's seal is unfurling its long wands of tiny bells, along with merrybells, *Uvularia grandiflora*, and the various lilylike fairy-bells, varieties of native and Japanese disporum. Primroses in yellow and white are at their peak. Violets are speckled with bloom. Native azaleas throw sweet fragrance into the air. This is the woodland at its peak.

By June we turn our backs on the woodland garden, distracted by lavish displays of flowers around the house, the roses and clematises along the fence lines, and the fresh rows of produce in the vegetable garden. But in the heat of summer, it is a place I retreat to, to sit on a bench or meander along its verges or kneel and weed a path. It is shadowy and green and cool, with ferns richly expanded, mounds of native sedge (*Carex pensylvanica*) softening the edges of the paths, and a quiet incident of flowering here and there—orchidlike toad lilies (the curious *Tricyrtis* family), native heucheras, the soft yellow *Salvia koyamae*. In fall, the native woodland asters, *A. cordifolius* and *A. divaricata*, are forgiven their colonizing ways as they open flower and weave a starry haze of white and blue beneath the trees.

THE VEGETABLE
AND CUTTING GARDEN

After the children were grown, the horses gone, a mammoth pile of manure no longer aging behind the barn (how I miss that manure!), I decided that this sun-filled spot at the northwestern end of the property would be perfect for a *real* vegetable garden, not the token patch I'd had before. I wanted satisfying rows of lettuces, leeks, broccoli, squash, beans, and peas. And cutting flowers. A place where I could grow annuals, no longer happy in my perennial-choked flower gardens—gaudy striped zinnias, little marigolds, gomphrenas, brown and pale yellow sunflowers, butter plate dahlias. I wanted a row of raspberries too, and a bed of strawberries, and nursery beds where I could try new plants to see if they were gardenworthy, as well as line out seedlings of biennials such as foxgloves for later inclusion in the borders.

I marked out an area sixty feet square and enclosed it with a split rail fence like those we had had for horses. Except in this case, I clothed the fence with chicken wire, and sank a foot of hardware cloth into the soil beneath the fence to discourage rabbits and any woodchucks that dared risk a brush with our dogs. On the advice of my friend the garden designer and artist Hitch Lyman, I dug a series of long beds that were no wider than four feet, so that you could reach across each bed without stepping on the soil and possibly compacting it. Compost and the last of the aged manure were worked into the beds. The paths I left dirt and covered with hay at first, although by midsummer I had a serious weed problem.

For the first year of the vegetable garden, ironically, I grew mostly flowers. In a moment of naïve enthusiasm that winter, I offered to do the flower arrangements for a friend's September wedding as my present to her. I needed all the extra room I could muster to grow the blooms, for we agreed to use no florist flowers—they were to come only from the garden or the wild. For structure (in the garden and in the bouquets), I planted the graceful *Hydrangea paniculata* 'Tardiva' in each of the four corners, knowing its conical spires, which appear on new wood, would be in full flower in September. White buddleias were planted along the fence, and sunflowers in all their vibrant shades of yellow, red, and brown, as well as the graceful, small-flowered, cream-colored 'Italian White'. Swaths of white cosmos and white summer phlox were added to the beds, as well as dahlias and zinnias in the hot colors my friend adored. These were mixed in the arrangements with goldenrod from the fields, ferns from the woods, tansy, rue, and sage from the herb garden, and long sprigs of sweet autumn clematis from one of our arbors. The resulting bouquets, made over the two days and nights before the ceremony, had a winsome and seasonal charm that might have been absent from a florist's gatherings of hothouse blooms.

To some extent over the following years, flowers made way for vegetables, although a visitor in high summer might see it otherwise. I cannot bear not to have stands of sunflowers, gaudy dahlias, and those plumes of white hydrangeas among the beans and tomatoes. Johnny-jump-ups and blue larkspur seed in the beds and paths, and I allow them to add their puddles of purple and blue in the spring as long as they don't interfere with other plantings. Some years, hollyhocks spring up in the outer beds and even in the paths, making it difficult to squeeze around them.

But, my, how charming they are in bloom, these tall spires of saucer faces in colors ranging from cream to pink to the deepest plum, nearly black! Two long beds on either side of the central path of the vegetable garden, the one that runs from the entrance gate to the chicken house at the opposite end, are given over to cutting flowers. I plant the front edge of these two beds with pansies and violas in the early spring in a gradation of colors that begins with yellows, then oranges and browns, deepening to blacks and purples, then washing to blues, becoming increasingly paler, ending finally with whites. It is my frivolous homage to Gertrude Jekyll and her famous English herbaceous borders of hot-to-cold coloration. When the violas begin to look ratty in late June, I pull them out and plug in nasturtium seeds for a pathway of the fiery colors I love in summer.

This spring I redesigned the vegetable beds in the garden. It was time. The boards originally used to edge the beds had rotted, and soil was spilling into the paths. The paths, I now

The vegetable garden

thought, were unnecessarily wide, a perfect breeding place for weeds; much better to narrow them down and have more room for vegetables. I decided to cut up the very long beds and make them slightly wider, throwing Hitch's advice to the winds, so that I could grow one sort of vegetable family in each, making the rotation of crops, which is so important to combat disease, simpler to manage. I left the two central borders for cutting flowers as is, as well as the outer bed that ran along the fence line, but all the other beds were fattened by a foot and divided into squares, five or six feet long, with narrow paths in between. Cedar planks, one inch by eight inches, were sunk halfway into the ground to edge the beds. Gravel, the small pale brown and gray pea gravel we use in the other gardens and on the driveway, was added to dress the paths.

I spent hours poring over Eliot Coleman's books on organic vegetable gardening, making lists, plotting my plantings. Then, on a piece of paper, I roughly drew the new series of beds—eight of them symmetrically placed on each side of the central cutting borders—then numbered them, one to sixteen, and segregated my vegetables: lettuces in one bed, root crops in another, and squash, brassicas, strawberries, peas, beans, onions, and the nightshade tribe (tomatoes, peppers, and eggplants), each in its own bed. Next year we will rotate each crop, except for the strawberries, which remain in place for at least three years. Leeks and onions will go where lettuces were, lettuces where peas and beans grew, brassicas in one of the tomato beds. The soil in the beds, if we remember, will be turned over in the fall with well-rotted leaves and some aged compost from the chicken yard. I find the squarer beds easy to weed, even if they are five feet across, since paths wrap around them on all sides. And the new regiment of small beds set in rows in gravel has a pleasing appearance—a friend said it looked very French— because of its orderly, geometric design.

The outer beds of the vegetable garden, along the split rail fence, are given over to a mishmash of plants. Japanese cucumbers climb the chicken wire, along with a purple morning glory and the charming sky blue bells of *Clematis* 'Betty Corning'. A few roses are here for cutting, and stands of perennial daisies, *Helianthus* 'Lemon Queen' and the willowy, late-blooming, pale yellow *H.* 'Sheila's Sunshine'. Several highbush blueberries are included, coaxed into fruit with some acid added to the soil in the guise of peat moss and pine needle mulch. A clump of serpent garlic, also called rocambole, unwinds its heads of tiny bulbils among racemes of apricot agastache and tiny scarlet zinnias, the species *Z. tenuifolia*. At the far west end, the fence is bordered with raspberries, some early, others fall-bearing.

I mentioned to Bosco that I wanted a chair in the garden (shouldn't every garden have a chair or bench for sitting?), and he lugged down an old beauty, cast iron, painted white, cut in floral curlicues, with a wraparound back and curvaceous legs. It seems an appropriate chair for this voluptuous place, and I do sit in it, to write on labels or just rest and look around. In late summer, when the gardens around the house are quiet, long past their June prime, and the woodland is green and dark and shadowy, all here is extravagant, wildly blooming and fruiting, vibrant with color. Squash leaves are four-foot umbrellas shading yellow crepe paper flowers and green-striped fruit that spill out of their prim beds; the bean vines weave up tuteurs eight feet tall, dripping scarlet flowers and pale green pods. Goldfinches come to drink rainwater from the cupped leaves of silphium and peck at the seed of sunflowers. Tomatoes, tied against A-frame wooden stands, pull heavily on their vines above glossy bushes of green and purple basil. Dahlias, single-petaled, in hues of red and orange, dance in the borders among dill and white cosmos, and the chickens cluck excitedly as I toss them weeds and bolting lettuce.

THE MEADOW

The newly planted meadow stands across a grass path from the barn and vegetable garden, bound on its south side by our ribbon of woodland. I think of it as our most tentative, unpredictable work in progress, thrilling in theory if not quite yet in fact.

I just came in from cutting down a wheelbarrow load of ragweed, its sneeze-inducing pollen scattering into the air as I did so, and stalks of wild lettuce in this meadow. The fleabane that appeared unexpectedly this spring and bloomed prettily in June is now brown and brittle and so tall it is obscuring the rudbeckias, monardas, and mountain mint that are in full flower. And where are those waving grasses that I long for? No, no, no, this is not how it is supposed to be. I am learning that it's not easy to have the meadow of your dreams. If you are fortunate enough to inherit a sunlit field already established with soft grasses and occasional wildflowers, count your blessings. For creating a native meadow in a place where one didn't exist is fraught with difficulties. It demands patience (we're talking years), close scrutiny, and diligent weeding.

Naïvely, I assumed otherwise. I thought all you had to do was stop mowing the grass more than once a year to achieve that waving landscape I cherish from childhood summers spent in New England. Not content with the distant view of hayfields just beyond the stone wall that marks the end of our property,

I yearned for a meadow of my own. So, after Bosco and I were married, I set about creating one in the old half-acre paddock below the barn, where we were now building a lap pool. I wanted no flower borders here, no pots to water, but instead, a meadow around the pool, high grass, black-eyed Susans, asters, orange butterfly weed, the wild lavender bergamot (*Monarda fistulosa*) that I catch glimpses of in fields around here. The paddock was originally seeded with a pasture mix, full of the timothy and alfalfa that horses love. With the horses gone, the pool finished, a ten-foot strip of lawn established around its stone edging for children to run on in bare feet, I simply let the surrounding pasture grass grow, determining to mow it once in late fall. For the first few years, grasses dominated, not native meadow grasses, but nonetheless tall and waving, and slowly a few asters and goldenrod moved in. But so, almost imperceptibly at first, did vetches and bindweed. Then the alfalfa began to take over huge swathes, pushing out the grasses. My meadow started to look like a weed patch. I pulled at the vines and tried digging out the alfalfa, but its roots went down to China, and finally I gave up, realizing I needed help.

I called Larry Weaner, the well-known designer of native meadows from Pennsylvania, and asked him if he would come for a consultation. I was familiar with two of Larry's creations—a ravishingly beautiful forty-acre meadow in northwestern Connecticut, and a smaller one, designed for neighbors within walking distance of Duck Hill, that I found enchanting, especially when masses of tall asters, in every hue of blue and pink and white, bloomed in October. Larry came, seemed to like our comparatively tiny site, its full sun and poor, sandy soil (just what you need, he said), and waxed poetic about the native meadow we could have: little bluestem grasses, turning russet and golden in the autumn, with a succession of wildflowers from spring through fall to attract birds and butterflies. I was hooked. The bad news, he gently informed me, was that we would need to use glyphosate (better known as Roundup) to kill the weedy plants that were there. Or, alternatively, cover the whole place with black plastic for a couple of years. I hated the thought of using a herbicide, even one, like Roundup, that doesn't linger in the soil. But I knew he was right that we had to get rid of the invasive plants that were there without disturbing the soil and thus activating even more weeds. The black plastic method was too hideous to contemplate. Brushing my reservations aside, I asked Larry to help me realize this dream.

Our half acre was carefully sprayed with Roundup in the fall, avoiding the few native wildflowers that existed as well as the wild species roses we had planted along the fence line. The following spring, after dabbing any lingering weeds with a second application of Roundup, Larry came with a crew of helpers, raked the debris off the field, and sowed the ground with waves of native grasses, sedges, and forbs (wildflowers). Larry had in mind a more varied palette than I envisioned, including flowers more common in the prairies of the Midwest than in a New England meadow. At first I wasn't sure I liked this idea, but then I decided, why not? The point was to have plants that were suited to the conditions we had to offer, mostly high and dry, with an area of moister soil where the land dipped toward the woods. His seed list included baptisia, asters, milkweeds, coreopsis (the native *C. tripteris*), eupatorium, mountain mint, bee balm, and goldenrods, as well as purple love grass and little bluestem. Several hundred plugs of perennials (amsonia, silphium, more asters, the lovely meadow phlox, *P. pilosa*) were added in drifts. We set up sprinklers and diligently watered our future meadow until the rains of autumn took over. I watched as seedlings came up in the warmth of summer, and also weeds, especially vast colonies of purslane, from which, at least, I gleaned some vitamin-rich salad fixings.

That was last year. This is the first real season of the meadow, and Larry warned me not to expect much. He says it takes three years for a seeded native meadow to come into its own, that the native grasses are slow to establish but eventually will take over from the weeds. I trust him. I have seen the results of his handiwork. And I was thrilled, this spring, to find colonies of the sweet red and yellow columbine, *Aquilegia canadensis*, flowering in the shadier edges of the meadow. All summer this flowering field has been alive with butterflies. Yesterday I watched as a flock of goldfinches landed on the swaying stalks of tall rudbeckias. The willowy biennial coneflower with tiny black-eyed Susan faces, *R. triloba*, is blooming in profusion where the meadow slopes down to our patch of woods. So is the six-foot-tall sunflower *Helianthus angustifolius*. I catch glimpses of the lavender bergamot. And yet I spy alfalfa cropping up here and there and wonder if the native grasses will be tough enough to push it out. Ailanthus seedlings pop up out of nowhere. Bindweed is back. Larry says not to dig up weedy interlopers, for that just disturbs the soil and activates more weed seeds. Instead, cut them down, or brush them with Roundup.

I'm going to be patient. I'm going to think positively. And after all, we are contributing a tiny bit to energy conservation by not having more lawn. No deafening, air-polluting blowers, no mowing except for once a year in early March. But I realize the meadow I hope to have is virtually another garden with a garden's needs—tending, weeding, editing. Maybe someday it will be beautiful without any effort on my part, naturally beautiful, but I somehow suspect it's not that easy.

THE SHAPING
OF THE GARDEN

DOORWAYS

On summer days, a gardening friend of mine throws open the French doors from the spare interior of his Long Island cottage to reveal a pathway plunging into a romantic tangle of roses, perennials, annuals, and fruit trees. It is all I can do to stand inside for the hellos and how-are-yous with a modicum of graciousness, I want so badly to walk through those doors out into this flowery wilderness. Doorways are often a logical place to begin when designing a garden. What you see from your doors becomes your garden's introduction, the first glimpse, the view that entices you outside. It might just be a bench directly across a lawn in the shade of an ornamental tree that catches your eye, or a path disappearing into a copse of trees, or the suggestion of a pattern of flower beds beyond a terrace. These doorway views not only lure you outdoors; they also visually connect the garden to the house.

Three doorways at Duck Hill were obvious launching pads for my garden schemes. The front door of our old farmhouse is useless as an entrance, opening into a hallway not much bigger than an icebox. I have a little desk and chair there in its nook, surrounded by paintings and photographs of family dogs, and there I pay bills, pile up notes to be answered, and occasionally write letters that are actually, archaically, in longhand. But if someone unused to our house knocks on the door, we are in trouble, for there is not enough room for the person who is opening the door and the person who is entering to coexist. This symbolic entrance door, placed symmetrically in the center of the prim south facade of the house, was the departure point for the axis that leads down painted wooden steps between two fat cubes of yew into the main garden. If you are standing at the front door, your eye travels through an opening in the privet hedge that shields this square garden, moves across the flowery enclosure and lawn, and out another gap in the privet to a teak bench placed between two Carolina silverbell trees. The bench is so lichen-encrusted now that it's an itchy place to sit unless you're dressed in thick jeans, so I think of it more as an object to stop your eye. A stone wall and a line of massive old sugar maples behind the bench mark the southern boundary of our property.

The porch door

The actual working entrance to our house, off to one side like an afterthought, is a door to what was once an open porch and is still so called. It is a narrow enclosed space, nine feet by twenty-one, brick-floored, and flooded with the light from floor-to-ceiling mullioned windows that line the north, east, and south walls. An old Oriental rug covers the center of the floor, but the rest is taken up by baskets and plants, lots of plants. It is, in fact, our garden spilling indoors. Bosco's collection of begonias resides here (he cannot resist a patterned leaf), staggered on two long tables that are somewhat shaded. In winter, strappy clivias join the begonias, eventually offering up their extravagant orange and yellow trumpets. Against the row of east windows, I stage fragrant white cyclamen in winter and cape primroses (varieties of streptocarpus) in summer on two old wrought-iron stands. Flowering bulbs are brought in to stand on the brick floor and tables for added color and fragrance. We keep the thermostat on this entrance porch at fifty-five degrees, but with sunlight the temperature rises to a comfortable warmth, and then I open the French doors that divide this entryway from our library.

Just outside the porch door, in the right angles of the porch, the library, and our bedroom wing, I made a small courtyard. This area was once our driveway and the bedroom our garage, but I hated having cars and delivery trucks parked right outside our windows. So the driveway was rerouted a good distance up the road and out of sight, the asphalt torn out, and generous holes dug for trees. A graveled walk now runs from the porch door out past two pairs of crab apples (the stellar 'Snowdrift' variety with single white flowers and an upright habit), each primly embraced in a square of boxwood hedging. The walk continues through an opening in the euonymus hedge that frames the courtyard, on past the grassy slope where we have dwarf apple trees, and into the new parking area, which is shielded from view by another clipped hedge, this time of cornelian cherry, *Cornus mas*. A white-flowering dogwood tree planted just beyond the parking area ends this axis. Bosco, who does the lion's share of our grocery shopping, at first complained about the distance he had to trudge with the groceries, down the gravel path from the parking area and through the porch and library to the kitchen, realizing, perhaps too late, that practicality was not his new wife's strong point. The problem was solved, or at least Bosco was appeased, by the arrival of a gift from a sympathetic son—an all-terrain-wheeled, shiny red, wooden-slatted wagon to carry the heavy bags.

From the entrance porch, you catch a glimpse of the outdoors at the other end of the house, through the library and the kitchen, where glassed French doors open out to the terrace and up three steps to the patterned herb garden. At the end of this garden, on axis with the kitchen doors, a rustic arbor twined with rambling roses shades yet another mossy bench. Because so much of our time is spent in the kitchen, cooking, eating, entertaining, this doorway and the aspect from it are perhaps the most important, since from here, we are beckoned into the garden. The kitchen doors are wide open all summer, and many of our meals are eaten out on the terrace at a round table in the shade of an old, graceful Japanese crab, *Malus floribunda*. When I first planted this crab apple, it was a spindly specimen and my children laughed when I said it was going to shade our alfresco lunches. Now, thirty years later, the children, of course, are grown and gone, but they return to eat beneath the tree, which forms a wide parasol over our table and in its picturesque architecture is a treasured feature of the garden at all seasons.

Because I love to walk by perfumed plants and have their sweetness waft indoors, the edges of the terrace are planted with shrubs that release their fragrance into the air—the lilac 'Miss Kim', *Viburnum carlesii*, and two scented daphnes, *D. cauca-*

sica, which blooms intermittently all summer, and the variegated *D. burkwoodii* 'Carol Mackie'. Pots staged on either side of the doorway and at the stone steps are planted with purple violas in the spring, scented geraniums in summer.

In the winter months, the view from the kitchen doors sustains us, keeping us connected to the garden. The kitchen is large and sunlit, jutting out into the terrace with an old behemoth of a stove at one side and shelves of crockery on the other. In the middle of this space, just in front of the French doors, six white-painted, mismatched wooden chairs surround a long wooden table, rescued from a shed on the property where I once lived. Here, many hours are spent lingering over meals.

On a cold December morning at breakfast, I look up into the herb garden, past great lumpy balls of boxwood to the dwarf blueberry hedge surrounding a circular stone water trough. The hedge is pleasing to see even now, though bare of leaves, for its prettily zigzagging twigs are rose-hued. Beyond the herb garden, an old bush of native winterberry, *Ilex verticillata*, is still studded with scarlet berries—one day soon, a flock of robins will come to feast and strip it of its fruit. Birds use the arbor at the end of the kitchen axis as a landing station and swoop down for a drink at the pool of water, which we keep from freezing in winter with an electric birdbath deicer, its cord concealed as best we can in the gravel and beds as it snakes its way to an outdoor outlet. In winter, the terrace furniture—a conglomeration of old white-painted wrought iron, cushioned for comfort—is put away, and a bird feeder hangs from the Japanese crab. I keep a bird book by the canisters of flour and sugar, and binoculars in a nearby drawer, for identification when feathered strangers come to dine. Squirrels and chipmunks vie for the seed, and, as we linger at the table, our three dogs sit at the French doors watching with spine-tingling interest their winter antics in the garden.

These three doorways radiating out to our garden in different directions, north, south, and west, offer different sights, different experiences. Collectively, they force us into constant intimacy with the garden, for with each entering and exiting we are obliged to walk down its paths, smell its smells, note its patterns of shape and texture, register its flaws, drink in its flowering.

PATHS

We don't use paths enough in American gardens. Of course we all have a path from the garage, or the parking area, to the kitchen door, and usually a more formal but less-used path to the front door. But we don't take advantage of paths sufficiently *within* our gardens or along the perimeters of our properties to suggest a journey, an adventure.

When I was a small child, I spent many holidays with my aunt at her tiny eighteenth-century cape on Main Street in Hingham, Massachusetts. An elderly woman (probably all of fifty years old) lived next door and had a garden I loved. As I remember, it had many narrow gravel paths that wove through riotous beds of flowers, and, as my aunt visited with her neighbor, I happily wandered there. I have had a weakness for gravel paths ever since.

My aunt, short in stature and wide of beam, dressed invariably in sturdy tweeds and no-nonsense lace-up shoes, led a life I came to emulate—a dog-enlivened world of the outdoors, of books and cooking, of sketching, painting, gardening. She too had paths on her property that I remember with fondness. A long narrow stretch of lawn rolled down from the back of her house with flower borders on one side, and on the other a cluster of trees. There, a shaded path dipped down into a wooded dell where drifts of spring flowers and bulbs had naturalized over the years. This secluded—and to me enchanting—walk led to a wooden gate that opened onto a wide sunlit field. From here, a mowed path through high grass led to a parcel of woods she owned—thirty acres of mature beech, pine, and oak—in which she had blazed many trails. My aunt's routine throughout her life was to take a walk in that wood every morning, accompanied by her two boisterous dogs, and it was on those walks that I first learned to identify wildflowers and birds. When my aunt died at the stout age of ninety-two, she left those thirty acres of woods to the town of Hingham, and I like to think of her neighbors on Main Street going out their back doors to take a stroll on her entrancing paths.

I am always delighted to see my grandchildren and the children of friends here at Duck Hill meandering along the paths in the flower gardens or vanishing down the woodland walk. It is this childlike sense of adventure that I think paths give to a garden. It doesn't matter if your garden beds are geometric, as most of mine are, or asymmetrical and waving. If you have a way to walk through them as well as around them, a sense of involvement, of losing yourself in the garden, occurs. And if you can make a walk all the way around the perimeter of your property, possibly screening the pathway with plantings of trees and shrubs, suddenly your yard seems much bigger and more intriguing. Too many of our American backyards are just large open spaces of lawn that can be taken in at one glance, and therefore, oddly, appear smaller and infinitely less interesting.

The possibility of turning a corner on a path or disappearing around a bend, and not knowing as you approach that bend quite what lies ahead, adds an element of mystery. Surprise—a sense of surprise—is to me one of the most important aspects of a successful garden, something the designers of the classical French gardens knew so well. At Vaux-le-Vicomte or at Courances, you have no idea as you stroll past the parterre gardens and ornamental pools that you will suddenly come upon a stretch of water, a tree-lined canal crossing in front of you, or a shaded allée that will lure you left or right. These surprises are hidden from view until you descend some steps or turn a corner. Vaux and Courances are on an impossibly grand scale, but we can bring home lessons from them. Here at Duck Hill, visitors are often surprised by the wide-open sunny meadow that appears at the end of our shadowy woodland walk. Or the unexpected sight of water as you turn left on the path through the tiny yellow garden and spy a narrow pool beyond the paddock gate.

Paths can be made of many different materials, and I think it is best to choose what suits your house and the atmosphere of your garden. Most of the paths closest to the house at Duck Hill are made of quarter-inch unwashed pea gravel of a soft, warm gray-brown. I chose gravel not only because I was fond of it (besides those childhood memories, I love its crunch), but because it is cheap compared to stone or brick, easy to lay, and unpretentious, which suits the simple nature of our old farmhouse. You need an edging when you use gravel to keep it out of the beds or off the lawn. We used old brick sunk on its long sides (which after a number of years gets crooked and needs to be straightened—not a terribly difficult task) or, in some cases, fieldstone, which is more apt to stay put. We scraped up any topsoil before we put the gravel down, but didn't prepare the bed in any other way, for the subsoil here is poor and sandy and works well as a base. You don't want to put gravel on top of rich soil or it will swim and ooze after a good rain. Another mistake often made with gravel is putting it down too thickly. This makes walking in it as hard as walking in dry sand at the beach. Lay it no more than an inch thick, preferably less. Will it be traipsed into the house? Yes, but not badly. Will weeds grow in it? Yes, but so, delightfully, will choice bulbs and perennials. In our patterned herb garden, scilla and puschkinia have jumped the curbs of the beds and seeded into the gravel, making puddles of blue in the early spring. The sweet, true-blue annual love-in-a-mist (*Nigella damascena*) comes back from seed every year in the pebbles, and stately verbascums that I allow to remain in the paths turn the garden into a yellow and white forest in late June.

In the gravel terrace below this garden, white corydalis seeds about in shady nooks and blooms from April to November. An early-flowering nepeta (the original, old *N. mussinii*) has abandoned the perimeter beds and naturalized in the gravel along with Johnny-jump-ups and the cream-flowered, button-headed *Scabiosa ochroleuca*. In the nasturtium garden, small orange poppies crop up in the stony ground and flower all summer, and the charming native red and yellow columbine refuses to grow in the beds, appearing shyly in the gravel paths instead. If you are a neatnik, all this wayward flowering will probably be unsettling. But to me, the unexpected occurrences such as these give a garden a certain magic.

Brick laid in patterns makes an elegant path, either alone or in combination with gravel, and is appropriate certainly for an old-fashioned garden as well as for modern ones. It is best to confine brick to flat surfaces, however, for brick walks can become dangerously slick in wet weather and treacherous in winter on a slope. Stone is handsome if it is natural to the area, of a color and texture that blends with the surrounding indigenous stone. I love the look of large granite slabs set in grass for an informal garden path in New England, where granite abounds.

Grass paths are often the easiest choice leading from one lawn area surrounded by flowers to another. And is there anything more appealing than a mowed path curving through a meadow of high grass? We have a small area of semidwarf apple trees to one side of the graveled entrance walk that I call the mini-meadow. It is just rough grass, planted with daffodils, but I let it get quite high in the early summer, and mow a four-foot-wide path to curve up through it to reach the back gardens. In a friend's charming garden in northern France, a birch grove was planted many years ago to recall her husband's Russian past. The grass is kept at six or eight inches high in the area around the grove, but a closely mowed walking path weaves through the trees, beckoning the visitor.

Grass paths that lead into gardens can get quite worn with multiple visitors. Ours look a little weary after a day of being open to the public, but some compost sieved on the lawn in April helps to revive it. We have unintentionally worn a path in the grass (I would not call it anything as fancy as a lawn) above the hedged-in gardens on our frequent walks to the barn and chicken house—a depression and thinning of the turf rather like the narrow paths the deer make in the surrounding fields with their routine grazing patterns. I like the look of it in this informal area, although it would make a true lawn aficionado shudder.

We spread wood chips on the meandering paths through our small woodland because we have them at hand from trees and branches that have been cut down. I don't love their initial raw coarseness and yellow-brown color, but with age they turn silver and blend innocuously into the woodland picture. I have seen shredded leaves used on shaded walks to good effect, and finely shredded bark. A friend who gardens just north of Boston uses pine needles on the paths through her woodland, infinitely appropriate and beautiful where pines and hemlocks grow in abundance, as they do at her place. Bare earth makes a perfectly natural informal path. I love the idea of bare earth paths in a vegetable garden, though unless they are heavily traveled they quickly become weedy. Their other disadvantage is a tendency to become oozy with mud when we have rain. A venerable gardener nearby made paths through her wet woods, where sweet-smelling clethra colonized and towered overhead, by ingeniously piling stacks of newspapers and old telephone books on the moist ground and covering them with leaves and moss. Wayne Winterrowd and Joe Eck covered the paths in their entrancing vegetable garden in Vermont with old newspapers and catalogs, which rot over the winter and are then disguised with fresh, sweet-smelling straw.

I think one thing to keep in mind is to avoid materials for paths that are a wildly different color than the natural colors around you. Do resist blinding white gravel and bright orange mulch. Unless, of course, your goal is a bold artistic statement, something you want to leap out at you, to startle, rather than blend in with your surroundings.

TERRACES, WALLS, AND STEPS

The beauty of terraces, as well as decks, is that they encourage you to leave the confines of your house and linger outdoors. But I have reservations about decks that float out into the air from houses built on sloping land. Although it can be thrilling to be perched high above the ground in the canopy of trees, to some extent these decks divorce you from the garden. You are trapped there, an observer rather than a player, with no easy way of walking out onto your land. Terraces, on the other hand, are part of the garden. You are immediately there, able to lean down and smell a flower or pull a weed, to wander off on a stroll. They are ideal outdoor rooms, obvious extensions of your house, a cozy place surrounded by green architecture or flowers, perhaps with a view, where you can sit secluded with a book or gather friends and family around a table or the barbecue.

The first thing we did when we moved to Duck Hill, besides building bookshelves against most of the barren walls, was to extend the galleylike kitchen to accommodate our large family. At that time, a rough slope dropped down from the north to the doors of the new kitchen, and, to solve the problem of drainage, we were advised to build retaining walls and level the ground in front of the doors. It was an obvious excuse for a terrace. A meticulously skilled local stonemason, Sam Corsi, whose ancestors had come here from Italy to help build the great aqueduct that fed water to New York City, took on the project. I loved to watch him craft the three-foot-high walls without cement, using rocks he found on the property and nearby fields, fitting them together like a jigsaw puzzle, always looking for good "faces" and lichened surfaces. The resulting terraced area within the walls, about eighteen by forty-five feet, was leveled and dressed with pea gravel, and large granite stones were placed as a broad step down from the kitchen's French doors.

I dug three-foot-wide beds along the base of the walls, dividing them from the gravel with bricks set on edge, and here, at first, I planted 'Seafoam' roses, boxwood, and daylilies. The roses are gone now after fifteen years of good service, replaced with fragrant daphnes. The boxwood bushes have fattened to a prodigious size. Daylilies continue to color the terrace in summer, and regale lilies rise through them and the daphnes to contribute their own sweet perfume. I wish, in retrospect, I had built a long wooden arbor set into the gravel just outside the kitchen doors those many years ago to shade us in the afternoons, for the western sun then is hot and glaring. But since I had planted a crab apple instead in one corner of the terrace, we content ourselves with this natural umbrella.

Stone steps cut into the terrace wall lead up to the herb garden on the west side and through the nasturtium garden toward the mini-meadow to the north. I cannot think of a flat space that occurs naturally at Duck Hill. Everything is on a slant. The house, like so many that were built in the nineteenth century, is nestled into a gentle hillside, which rises at the back of our property, north and west, to an open field with a lovely view of hills. It was the sight of those distant hills and that field that convinced me so many years ago to move here. Most plants love an incline, especially if the land slopes to the south, as it does in most of our garden areas here, providing some protection from the wind, good drainage, and a maximum of sun. But, as in the case of the kitchen terrace, certain areas of the garden seemed to require flat spaces, and consequently the land was pushed a bit over the years, and steps and small walls proliferated. All the walls and steps have been laid dry, that is, without cement, just as the old farm walls were constructed here in the nineteenth century. Not only do dry walls look infinitely more appropriate in our countryside, they are better able to withstand the vagaries of our winters, the repeated freezing and thawing, with no rigid cement to heave and crack. When building steps, I've learned it is best not to make the risers too steep, no more than six or seven inches high. There is something horrifying as you get older about plunging down steps a foot or more deep, hoping your knees are not going to give

The kitchen terrace

out. The treads, on the other hand, need to be generous, at least a comfortable twelve inches, twice as broad as the risers. That way, a large foot has ample surface to climb or descend.

There is much to say for different levels in a garden. They add interest, diversity, and, again, the desirable element of surprise. The gardens of Italy enchant us with their terraced hillsides, each succeeding level, as we descend, revealing its pool of water, a fountain perhaps, embraced in a pattern of green hedges, vases of flowers staged on its balustrade, and, inevitably, a view beyond. In San Francisco, narrow gardens rise steeply behind Victorian houses, with paths and steps winding up through groves of camellias and magnolias, or wonderfully sculptural succulents. The garden at Dumbarton Oaks in Washington, D.C., designed by our great Beatrix Farrand at the beginning of the twentieth century, is Italianate in style and yet at home in its setting, terraced down a plunging hillside, with brick paths and steps leading you this way and that to a series of small, charming formal gardens, each a surprise, and on finally to a meandering wooded walk flushed blue with scilla in early spring.

On a much more modest scale, the various steps and walls, twists and turns, gravel paths and terraces at Duck Hill also add to the appeal of the garden. Perhaps, as my friend and colleague Wayne Winterrowd suggested, they give it a little European air, although to me it seems a very American garden, a hybrid of influences and styles adapted to its particular setting.

HEDGES

I am an unapologetic champion of hedges. They bring clarity, order, variation, and romance to a garden space. They can transform a blank expanse of green or gravel by dividing it into separate areas offering different experiences, contributing to a sense of surprise and seclusion. They are effective screens against road traffic or neighbors who live too close for comfort. They can be clipped to a strict geometric line or a rolling wave, or left to grow naturally in billows. They are easy to plant as young rooted specimens, take less time than you think to grow, are infinitely cheaper than walls and more interesting than fences. They offer mass, form, texture, and color throughout the year. Sometimes, as a bonus, they flower and fruit. All this hedges do at Duck Hill, shielding parking areas and the road, edging terraces, spilling over walls, defining and enclosing the small garden rooms that extend from the old farmhouse on all sides and dress it like a necklace.

Since colonial days, hedges were a mainstay of old gardens on the East Coast, inspired by a European tradition still very much alive today. But sometime in a young twentieth century, driven by a spirit of American openness as well as a love affair with lawns and lawn mowers, we slipped out of the habit of using hedges. It is almost as though we became afraid to be individuals, to separate our yards and gardens from those around us, to cut up open space and claim some privacy and an inde-

View to hemlock garden

pendent aesthetic. What would the neighbors think? American property owners in suburbia were bound by a communal rule of transparency that required a stretch of unfettered lawn from house to street, divided only by a driveway, from one neighbor to the next.

I see a change now, a movement away from communal openness, evidence of a desire for individual expression. Some brave souls are turning their front yards into flowering meadows, sometimes in the face of neighbors' protests. Others, in the drought-stricken West, have replaced their lawns with a tapestry of succulents nestled among gravel and rocks. Homeowners here in the Northeast increasingly crave privacy, and, since many towns have rules limiting the height of walls and fences along streets, they've begun to plant hedges. Inevitably, they choose evergreens to shield their houses and yards—yews, hemlocks, rhododendrons, white pines, arborvitae—all of which make successful screens where deer are not a menace. But in areas like ours that are infested with hungry deer herds, these evergreen barriers are quickly diminished to tufts on stilts unless they are clad with wire or plastic armor.

Boxwood remains one evergreen so far spurned by deer, and, as a hedge in the one-to-five-foot range, it lends a romantic, old-time air to the garden. Our next-door neighbors have head-high bushes of *Buxus sempervirens* lining their driveway, and from it you have no idea of the garden concealed behind them. We use the sturdy Sheridan hybrid boxwood 'Green Mountain' at Duck Hill to enclose the small white garden and one of our terraces, and hardy *B.* 'Vardar Valley' to frame the four crab apples in the front courtyard. 'Green Mountain' has a natural pyramidal shape and will grow to four feet or more without pruning. 'Vardar Valley' is more horizontal in growth and serves well as a two-foot hedge. Both of these varieties withstand our winters without protection, though we are careful to brush heavy snow off them. 'Green Mountain' and some of its boxwood kin are susceptible to box leaf miner, but if you shear the bushes a week after first seeing the little hovering flies in May, you will destroy the eggs these culprits have just laid on the tips of new growth, which would otherwise hatch and bury into the small oval leaves. Generally, though, when we are not combating these little insidious worms, we clip our box hedges the first week in June, preferably just after a rain.

When I first came to Duck Hill, the lawn that stretched south and east from the front door of the house spilled right out into the street, divided merely by a line of railroad ties, no longer slick with creosote but rough and battered, laid down haphazardly as if as an afterthought. It was a quiet rural street with more passing horseback riders than cars, but I wanted a pronounced separation between the garden and the road as well as a backdrop for the flowery borders I was planting. Thinking evergreen, I chose our graceful native hemlock, knowing that it would grow to considerable height and could be clipped or left unclipped. In those days, the woolly adelgid was not yet the threat that it has now become to hemlocks all over the Northeast, and deer were not devouring our evergreens as they do now. The three-foot-high conical trees that I planted flourished, growing over the years to ten feet in height, and now require a tall ladder or the back of a pickup truck for the light shearing we give them yearly in August. So far, we have not been troubled by the adelgid, but I keep an eye out for the telltale fuzzy white balls on the hemlocks' needles and know to spray with a horticultural oil if we see any. We clothe the hedge from late fall to spring with netting on the street side to discourage the deer, for although hemlock is not a favorite food, they will eat it in the dead of winter. I am not sorry I planted hemlock so many years ago. If unravaged by deer, it makes a handsome soft-textured hedge. But if I were doing it over again, I think I might choose a deciduous tree for this hedge instead, something like beech.

I am partial to deciduous hedges. They are often as effective at screening as evergreens, although we would expect otherwise. They are much less expensive to buy, are not caviar to deer, and offer a variety of interest through the seasons with their foliage, flowers, fruit, and branching. Naturally grown, unclipped hedges can be beautiful barriers or serve as a bold stroke of one color and texture where there is space for them to flourish. Along the road here, where we don't have hemlock, we've used our native cranberry bush, *Viburnum trilobum*, as a screen. It has a rounded shape and matures at about six feet, with maplelike leaves and white lacy flowers in May, followed by dripping clusters of glossy red berries that remain through fall and much of winter. For that stroke of one texture and color, I've planted a hedge of burnet roses at the top of a fieldstone wall along the south front of the barn. Here the bristly three-foot cinnamon-colored stems sucker into colonies and fountain gracefully over the face of the wall. Masses of fragrant white flowers are followed by hips the color of plums, and the rose's ferny foliage turns tawny hues in the fall. The hedge needs no care at all.

Lilacs make splendid informal hedges—choose the lovely six-foot 'Miss Kim' with ice blue flowers in late May and coppery foliage in October, or the taller-growing, graceful Chinese lilac, *Syringa* × *chinensis*, with masses of delicate purple trusses. The dwarf Korean lilac, *S. meyeri* 'Palibin', will make a dense hedge to five feet with its tightly branched habit and tiny leaves. Knowing that it can also be sheared beautifully (it is often trained into standard topiaries), we have tried it as a clipped hedge around our herb garden. It scents the air in May with its mauve-purple flowers, turns a burnished hue in the fall, and, I hope, will eventually be a four-foot geometric frame to contain the unruly herbs in this garden. We clip it after it blooms, and then go over it lightly several times during the summer to keep the desired horizontal line.

If forsythia is given the room to fountain, it serves as a densely twigged hedge that blazes in flower. But it is so overused, so hackneyed, it is hard to love it anymore—that is, unless it is used in an unusual way. I have an architect friend who massed forsythia in a line on either side of his driveway and then sculpted the bushes hard with shears into mounding clouds. It is a stunning piece of artwork, neon-yellow in April, rolling green in summer, and a dense curving mass of ginger twigs in winter, a favorite hangout for cardinals, he says.

Hedges are being used in exciting new ways in modern design, taking an old tradition and doing something different with it, as my architect friend has. The contemporary Dutch garden designer Piet Oudolf clips beech and yew hedges into a series of slanting, swooping theatrical curtains as a backdrop and contrast to his wildly beautiful garden of swaying meadow plants. The great Belgian landscape architect Jacques Wirtz teaches us to think of hedges as sculptures. He snakes clipped boxwood in sensuous curves along his flat canvas of lawn, for instance, just for the beauty of its form and the shadows it casts.

If you are going to use hedges to divide your garden into areas, and space is limited, clipping is probably advisable to keep them contained. It is wise, then, to choose a plant that doesn't grow too quickly. The all too familiar privet, left unclipped, will grow to a considerable height—ten or more feet—offering scented (some would say stinky) white flowers and blue-black fruit. When beautifully sheared as you see it in the mild seaside climate and rich soil of the east end of Long Island, it appears quite glamorous, a great billowing barrier that holds the garden behind it secret. But privet has to be trimmed every week or two through spring, summer, and fall if its sculptural form is to be maintained. And unless you've been careful to cant the sides of the hedge out as you go down—think of a gumdrop or an A-frame—you will end up with a leggy hedge. We have an embarrassingly leggy privet around the main garden and struggle to correct it, periodically cutting it back hard in early spring, lopping off some of its branches close to the ground in order to encourage them to bush out. Privet is a high-maintenance hedge, and if I had the energy, physical and mental, I'd pull it out and replace it with something else. What I've learned the hard way over the years is that fast growers like privet are not as desirable as slow-growing candidates when it comes to a hedge you intend to keep clipped.

You cannot do better than plant the small shrubby tree cornelian cherry, *Cornus mas*, for an easily maintained hedge from four to ten feet high. It is, I think, my favorite deciduous hedge at Duck Hill, and I wish we had it around the main garden instead of privet. We admire it daily where it frames our parking area on three sides, hiding the cars from view. Cornelian cherry has the beautiful ribbed leaves typical of dogwoods, tiny puffs of acid-yellow flowers that stud the branches in March, and glossy red fruit in late summer. The dense twiggy growth of its gray branches is appealing in winter. It is slow-growing but shapes up nicely, and needs to be clipped lightly only four times a year. Plant the individual plants four feet apart to make a hedge, and, no matter how much you don't want to, cut it back to half its growth the year after planting to encourage it to bush out from the bottom.

For a bold, high hedge, from six feet to forty, in full sun or partial shade, do consider the handsome European beech, *Fagus sylvatica*. Bosco and I have just planted a line of three-foot rooted beech saplings along one side of the back property at his small house in the French countryside, and dream of its eventual effect. A beech hedge's silver-gray trunks and branches are clothed with glossy green leaves in spring and summer that turn first gold and then coppery brown in fall and continue to cling on the branches through winter. The old leaves drop just as the new fresh green leaves emerge in spring. Hornbeam, *Carpinus betulus*, is similarly elegant, with a slightly more airy lacing of leaves, which turn yellow in fall and are shed in winter. Beech and hornbeam hedges are common sights in northern Europe, and inexpensive small plants are readily available there in the most common nurseries. Here, liner plants of beech and hornbeam are infinitely harder to find. In fact few hedge materials are widely available beside the ubiquitous privet, euonymus, and barberry. We, as customers, need to demand a wider and more refined variety of choices.

Because it is dependable, good-looking, and easily found in nurseries, *Euonymus alata* 'Compacta', like privet, is over-used as a natural or sheared hedge. It is cheap to buy, not bothered by pests or diseases, colors a vivid red-pink in autumn, and clips beautifully. We have a substantial frame of it around our front courtyard, planted years ago before I realized that this Asian euonymus was invasive, encroaching on the verges of our local deciduous woodland. For now, we will leave it and enjoy its geometry against the picturesquely twisted branches of crab apples within its confines.

One of the effects of clipped hedges I most depend on is their ability to bring structure, a sense of order, to an otherwise wild and chaotic collection of plants. Those sharp horizontal lines play nicely off the graceful crabs and waving grasses and bulging perennials in our various garden rooms. A certain visual tension is achieved when clipped geometry frames wildness, a pleasing contrast of formal and informal. It is the yin and yang of the garden.

PUNCTUATION
AND REPETITION

The great Gertrude Jekyll warns us not to spot plants in the garden like buttons on a waistcoat, and yet I find I have done exactly that with boxwood, and I like the effect. I've marked the entrances of each garden with solitary bushes of box, marched them down paths, and plunked them on either side of doorways. What started as small affordable boxwood balls, a foot at most in dimensions, sometimes mere rooted slips, are now, years later, great mounded behemoths, chest-high in most cases, sometimes head-high, and I realize they have, almost unintentionally, become a leitmotif of the gardens around the house. With their repetition, they lead your eye and foot from one small enclosure to the next and forcefully tie all their parts together. They punctuate the spaces, sometimes outrageously, adding weight and architecture to the enclosures throughout the seasons. In winter, their rich evergreen dress relieves the gray-brown twiggy starkness of the garden.

Their weighty presence is now a welcome contrast to the wild flowering that occurs much of the year in these garden enclosures. Like the strictly linear hedges, the sculptural mass of the box bushes contrasts pleasingly with the arching and swaying of flowering trees, shrubs, and perennials. This contrast could have been achieved with other evergreens—yew, for instance, or juniper. But I thought boxwood was most appropriate to the old-fashioned quality of these gardens and the house. And, as noted, they are not loved by deer, which was surely a consideration when I first planted them, before we surrounded the garden with a deer fence.

In the case of the tiny nasturtium garden, the series of box bushes have become its most important element. I innocently planted six pairs of *Buxus* 'Green Velvet' along the central path of this garden when it was first laid out fifteen years ago. 'Green Velvet' is lower-growing than 'Green Mountain' and is said to mature at about three feet by three feet, perfect, I vaguely thought, to balance the swaying daylilies and small shrubs in this hot-colored room. I didn't think through just how much space three feet by three feet would be in this very small garden. In fact, the bushes of 'Green Velvet' have spread to a fat four feet across the beds and out into the central gravel path. To my delight, they have become great characters all by themselves, not really balancing anything at all. The path, now, is so narrow that in wet weather you have to draw yourself up to your thinnest dimensions to pass through the box bushes without getting wet. Two years ago, I asked my daughter Kim, here with her family for a visit, to tackle them with her marvelously inventive eye and a pair of sharp shears. She is an artist, normally a sculptor in ceramics, and creates wonderfully fanciful "bushes" out of clay. With great gusto, she went after the overgrown box bushes as though they were artworks, stopping every few minutes to stand back and assess her progress. She shaped the pairs at the two entrances of the garden like plump upturned bowls, but the four middle bushes she clipped into cubes topped by rounded caps, stolid creatures with hats on. I think they give the garden its soul. The flowers around these green statues, once so important, are now merely fleeting incidents. In May and June, tiny orange poppies sway briefly against the box bushes' heavy, dense breasts before dropping their fragile, crepe paper petals. Later, in June and July, Asiatic lilies shoot up for a moment's glory above their densely rounded heads, opening tiers of flared back, flaming flowers. Off and on through spring and summer, gold and blood-red daylilies dance around their solid green skirts. But it is the box bushes alone that give this garden personality at all times of year.

I have purposely repeated other plants in the gardens around the house. Crab apples are a recurring punctuation, in the entrance courtyard, shading the kitchen terrace, marking the four corners of the main garden. Nepeta, that sprawling sort called 'Six Hills Giant', edges the four central beds of the herb garden, and when it blooms in June is a repeated haze of lavender-blue seen from the kitchen door. The lovely white *Iris tectorum* 'Album' is clustered at the borders' edges where the long central axis ends in the hemlock garden. This year I added the iris to the edges of the opposite beds at the entrance to this garden, repeating the sword shapes of its leaves and pale flowers in May.

Violets are a repeated theme along our woodland path—for aren't these most common (some would say weedy) plants, with their clumps of dark green, heart-shaped leaves, handsome throughout the growing season? And when they bloom in shades of purple and blue, cream white and rose pink, aren't they enchanting? I suppose you could say in the case of the violets that I am repeating drifts of a plant, a practice Miss Jekyll would approve. Clumps of hellebores are spotted all along the paths, and I hope that they will eventually seed enough to make great pools of nodding speckled flowers and finely cut leaves where they are planted. Creating drifts and waves of one plant is always a good plan, but spotting a plant like buttons on a shirt can be visually pleasing too, drawing you along on a garden adventure.

A HUSBAND
IN THE GARDEN

DISRUPTION

Having a husband is all very well, but a husband in the garden is a mixed blessing. I have been married most of my adult life, but not to anyone interested in digging in the earth. The garden was my world, rich with endless possibilities and paths of learning, where I plunged in, experimented, stumbled, and sometimes succeeded, alone. When a particularly fine sweep of a plant or a beautiful incident occurred, either by happenstance or my contrivance, I could call on my family to come and admire. After the required praise, they went back to their interests and left me at peace in my beloved, challenging, ever-consuming, flowery, leafy playground. Then I married Bosco, a gardener. Suddenly I was to share this plot, welcome another eye, another sensibility.

At first I was possessive, rigid, suspicious. It was difficult for Bosco. With boundless enthusiasm and a real love of plants, he tried valiantly to contribute to this established garden. But his every move was suspect. "Who planted that there?" I would ask, returning home from a speaking engagement. Bosco's shoulders would hunch as I looked down, say, at a small drift of red-striped yellow tulips (*Tulipa chrysantha*) in the hemlock garden where all is—or was—purple, mauve, magenta, and cream. "But aren't they pretty," he offered sheepishly. Well, yes, of course they are. This tiny species tulip is irresistible in its jauntiness. "Not here" was my stern reply. No. It was not my vision, my plan; the bulbs had to be moved.

Bosco has loved gardens and gardening all his life. As a small child, he wandered contentedly in the walled kitchen garden of his family's estate in Hungary, and as a young adult he escaped the elegant stone of Paris, where he lived with his young family, to dig and plant on weekends in a half-acre garden at a converted farmstead near Fontainebleau. When I met him in the nineties, he was a widower, and lived in a stone gatehouse on the Hudson where he spent happy hours tending another small garden. These gardens were a hodgepodge of plants, but it didn't matter. What Bosco loves is the *action* of gardening, the starting of seed, the rooting of cuttings, the growing of plants, the nurturing. He was never particularly interested in an overall effect. He says he's not a visual person—although he is a master at hanging pictures and noticing details about people.

When I started gardening passionately as a young married woman, I too was engrossed in the growing and tending of plants, a pleasure that absorbs me still. But I had an artist's background, having drawn and painted all my life and studied the history of art, and a temperament that was more expressive, more romantic, than practical. Very quickly I wanted to paint pictures with plants. I began, almost unconsciously, to think of the garden as a series of canvases, combining color and texture, mass and silhouette. Several decades later, I am still trying to achieve pleasing vignettes in the various parts of the garden, a succession of delightful moments captured, no matter how fleetingly, through the days and weeks and months of the garden's year.

Settling into our marriage, Bosco and I are slowly, at times painfully, learning the art of compromise. Bosco now invariably announces when he is going to plant something in case I might screech, or urges me to come show him just where I think a plant should go. And I am able quite often to admit delight at his surprise contributions, and sigh with relief at the energy and industry with which he plants bulbs and perennials when I am busy writing or traveling.

For a few years before I knew Bosco, I was so busy seeing and writing about other people's gardens that the garden here became rather tired and neglected. That has changed. Bosco's enthusiasm rekindled mine, and together we've tackled the refurbishment of old areas and launched into new gardening projects. It is a joint effort, and the results, the good incidents, the thrilling moments, and the knotty problems are gladly shared.

A garden is most often a place of solitude and reflection, and with that in mind, we tend to go off on our separate ways to work in it. The greenhouse is Bosco's domain, and growing plants from seed and cuttings his special pleasure. The one drawback, I find, is his inability to throw anything away. Come the middle of May, he appears with trays and trays of successfully grown seedlings, which I am then expected to find room for in the already bulging garden. We jam in nicotianas and salvias wherever a crack is revealed in the flower beds, plunge scented geraniums willy-nilly into the herb garden, and fill the vegetable garden with a bounty of tomatoes and peppers (he is Hungarian after all), as well as sometimes dubious perennials or annuals that have caught his fancy. The extras—and there are always extras—are, to my relief, given away to willing friends.

Bosco now oversees our collection of dahlias, some of which, like the winsome 'Bishop's Children', he has raised from seed. The dahlias are saved, of course, from year to year, dried out after frost in the autumn, stored over winter in the garage neatly labeled and buried in peat moss or vermiculite in Styrofoam boxes, hauled out of their winter beds every spring, and planted in the long cutting beds of the vegetable garden at the end of May. As the tubers multiply every summer, here too he ends up with many to give away. He fusses over our collection of clematises (which weave in and out of the shrub roses and ramblers along the paddock fence), pruning and feeding them with wood ashes, and compost in the spring. Early in the year, he tackles the culling of deadwood from our shrubs and roses,

Clematis × *triternata* 'Rubromarginata'

pollards our purple smokebush, and saws to the ground any old unproductive branches in our forsythia and lilacs. All spring and summer, he plants and cares for the many pots that we stage around the garden.

I, meanwhile, do the bulk of the weeding, something I enjoy despite my aching knees. The results of my labor are instantly realized, edges crisped, plants unfettered, soil stirred. And all the while, I am refamiliarizing myself with every small detail of the garden, occasionally standing back to see the whole of it, looking, editing, ditching a thug here, allowing an unexpected cropping up of plants there, extending a sweep of something pretty that pleases the eye. Throughout our day of separate work, we long to share our discoveries and dilemmas, our achievements and thoughts, and so we call to each other periodically, to come and see, to consult, to admire. This is the pleasure of being married to another gardener.

ONE OF EVERYTHING

When the passion of gardening first hit me, I couldn't afford to spend much money on perennials. So I bought one each of whatever I wanted, and after a year or two divided it. Few perennials don't benefit from frequent division—peonies and fraxinella (*Dictamnus*) are rare exceptions—and over the years, I divided and divided again, eventually achieving a mass of one plant. Interwoven sweeps of plants, I soon realized, had a powerful impact visually, bold strokes of color and texture that created the painterly impression I was after in the garden.

Certain plants, without any help from me, have spread on their own, resulting in substantial swaths. Some of these are out-and-out thugs, whose advance requires yearly checking—violets, some native asters, comfrey, and fern-leaf tansy, for instance—but other perennials expand quietly over the years, finally becoming a presence in the garden. Boltonia is one of these, slowly bulking up to a sizeable girth, now, to my unexpected delight, a showstopping froth of delicate white asterlike daisies in September. Their narrow, blue-green leaves on upright stems remain in good health, requiring no care through our volatile summers. *Amsonia tabernaemontana*, which I planted many years ago in two small patches in the main garden, has also expanded, growing ever bigger with billows of lance-leafed stems, starry with sky blue flowers in spring and a soft blaze of gold in October. I am thrilled it has gained enough ground to make a statement, for this drought-tolerant native perennial has a beautiful habit and stellar foliage throughout the summer.

Bosco doesn't see it that way. What he longs for is plants, a variety of plants, one of each is just fine, and those voluminous clumps of amsonia, like a host of other lusty perennials, haven't left much room in the beds for newcomers. So he complains that there is too much amsonia, why would you want so much amsonia, it's so dull (he says this in July when its foliage, unfazed by disease or pest or drought, merely lends a quiet feathery texture to the garden). We need, he says, to plant other plants, new plants, different plants.

At first I muttered bitterly to my new husband that he wanted to hack away anything doing well enough to have a visual impact so he could have his one treasured this and treasured that. But he had a point. Our struggle was between two worthy notions: one, the effect of massing a plant, its calmness, its visual power, and its sense of lavishness; the second, variety in the garden, adding richness of detail, the excitement of the new and unknown, with the possibility of painting new, fresh brushstrokes in the future. In time, we sorted it out.

Bosco says that now he's learning to appreciate the effectiveness of sweeps of plants and the essentialness of good foliage in the garden, and, in turn, I admit that a few new perennials and annuals add some sorely needed spice to the gardens. We can at least *stop* the amsonia from advancing farther. While we're at it, we could back up the Joe-Pye weed, which wants to take over in rich moist soils, maybe moving it to the lower part of the meadow, and cull some of the mildew-ridden summer phlox that has seeded, reverting to its natural pasty blue-pink.

I have even painfully admitted that maybe we have too much *Helianthus* 'Lemon Queen'. I love this long-blooming, graceful, hardy sunflower, and have said repeatedly to Bosco in

Helianthus 'Lemon Queen'

reply to his complaints that as far as I was concerned the more the better. It is another billower, about four feet in height, and the abundance of small clear-yellow daisy flowers creates a splendid show all August and September. How many perennials bloom for that length of time? Butterflies like it, and goldfinches, my favorite summer bird, often land on the swaying stems to eat the seeds. But, yes, all right, it is taking over, in two separate areas. We have it planted at the west entrance to the small yellow garden, and in high summer, it is now getting difficult to enter and exit here without getting whipped in the face by its flowering stems. It is also getting uncomfortably close to the roots of some precious roses nearby—the early, muddled 'Harrison's Yellow' and the very fragrant, white-flowering alba 'Mme Legras de St. Germain'. In the vegetable garden,

'Lemon Queen' has naturalized (Bosco would say that's a nice way of putting it) along the south and east fence lines where we grow cutting flowers and some vegetables. It gives this garden a wild, voluptuous atmosphere in summer that I love. But my husband is right—we have little room left for anything else, and we both yearn to grow more vegetables. Some of it (emphasis on the *some*) must go.

I have always clung to the old and familiar and been wary of new ideas. Bosco helps me get over that. The collector's fascination with the new and out-of-the-ordinary infects me too, and now, each year, we manage to find room for a few unfamiliar plants. Some are noted as disappointments, eventually pulled out because they look bitsy, or have little to recommend them in flower or habit. Others falter in our sandy soil or vanish with the harshness of our climate. (We are designated as USDA Zone 6a now, though fifteen years ago we were Zone 5.) A few, however, are prized, sometimes conversation pieces among fellow gardeners. One such plant is the tall white burnet, *Sanguisorba tenuifolia* 'Alba', in the white garden. The foliage is exemplary, a two-foot-high clump of intricately cut dark green leaves. The flowers are odd and wonderful, crooked fingers of white fuzz that rise on tall willowy stems in late June and early July. This is a see-through plant that can be planted near the front of the border, for even though the flower stalks reach a height of five feet, they are so airy and delicate that you can see right through them to the plants behind. To make room for the burnet, we thinned out an ever-increasing stand of *Iris sibirica*, an iris I love for its tiny white-and-yellow-flecked blooms that I brought to Duck Hill from my previous home, where it was naturalized in a field. But it is aggressive, wanting to take over the entire garden, and it is in flower for half a minute.

The four-foot-tall tufted hair grass, *Deschampsia caespitosa*, bought recently from a mail-order nursery on the strength of its description, turns out to be an elegant addition to the main garden, adding a bold linear pattern of arching dark green leaves to the front of one border—a decided improvement over the unintended patch of summer phlox that had seeded there. In early summer, this grass is clouded with fine, feathery seed heads that bend prettily and sway in a breeze. There was a time, early in the garden's life here, when I resisted the inclusion of grasses in the flower borders, thinking them more appropriate to the edges of ponds and pools. I was wrong. Ornamental grasses, planted singly or in a wave in garden beds, are remarkably effective, their graceful upright lines and movement offering a visual relief from the stouter, rounder perennials that dominate.

I am enchanted with the low-growing aster *A. oblongifolius* 'October Skies', a haze of lavender-blue. We first saw this fine perennial a few autumns ago planted in sweeps in the Battery Conservancy garden at the tip of Manhattan. We jotted down its name and ordered a plant or two of it the following spring. Now I have divided this stellar perennial to extend its color along some of the edges of the main garden. What was discarded? Some floppy catmint, *Nepeta* 'Six Hills Giant', which was killing the grass (this is a plant better in gravel or along a wall or stone edging), and ever-increasing clumps of lady's mantle that definitely needed some culling.

LABELS

There was a time when I knew every plant in my garden by name, both its correct Latin nomenclature and its more colorful common name. I carefully recorded newcomers in my garden notebooks, where I planted them and when, described their characteristics, even crossed them out, with the date, if they died, which a shocking number did. Because I have a visual memory, this record was fixed in my mind. The fact was, I had an aversion to labels. They were a distraction, I thought, in a home garden. In botanical gardens, I rely on them, for I go there to learn like everyone else. But I didn't want to see sticks with names in my borders.

Then life intervened. Upheaval, divorce, travel, distraction. I stopped being meticulous about recording new plants, which were often unexpected gifts from friends. I began to lose track of what was in the garden. Visitors would ask me the name of some new perennial or annual and, to my horror, I wouldn't always know. I felt like a fool and vowed to be get back to keeping my journals.

With Bosco's arrival, all was lost. Busy with a new life and expanded family, I continued to be sloppy about recording new denizens in the borders. And I had married a gardener with a collector's appetite and no talent for remembering plant names. Labels started appearing in the garden, white plastic labels stuck about like little gravestones. I shrieked and muttered, and finally groped for a compromise. If we have to use labels, I said, what about wooden ones that would at least blend in with the soil? So the little white plastic sticks were replaced with wood, which promptly disintegrated over the first wet winter. Come spring, we would squint at their remains, hopelessly trying to read what we had written. Back to plastic labels (green ones, I found, were less objectionable than white) pushed into the dirt behind the plant in question, to be probed for and dug out with our fingers to read when challenged with the forgotten name.

Mystery shrubs met a better solution. Bosco was baffled by our viburnums, for I had collected many varieties and cultivars that were unfamiliar to him. So, with a pencil, I indented small rectangular metal tags with their Latin names and tied their wire ends to a branch of each bush. Other shrubs and even some small trees now have their metal labels, discreetly hanging from a twig, and I confess to peering at these labels quite often myself to remind me of a certain species or cultivar.

The woodland garden is actually an essential place for some identifications. The spring ephemerals such as anemones, jeffersonias, and corydalises vanish after blooming, and unless there is some marker, it's easy to forget their location and innocently plant something else on top of them. And it is the only way we can keep track of the various disporums, hellebores, primroses, epimediums, and trilliums we can't resist bringing home from nurseries. I tried stiff metal labels at first, the ones with wire prongs, but they get bent (who steps on them?) or pulled (chickens, dogs?), and somehow end up nowhere near the plant they're supposed to be identifying. I now resort to those cursed plastic labels shoved deep into the soil, or rely on our records, better kept now, and just hope I'll remember which is which and where.

Does it matter if you don't know the names of your plants? No, of course it doesn't. If you love certain plants, love their color and pattern, texture and fragrance, you don't need to

know what they are called. Unless you enjoy learning their ti-
tles and nicknames, or happen to want to write about them, as
I do, or are embarrassed when someone asks you what a flower
in your garden is and you can't remember. Bosco is fascinated
with the origin of names—who were Mr. Forsyth and Mr. Clive,
Betty Corning and Cedric Morris? And it is fun to learn of their
provenance.

VARIEGATED PLANTS

Once I spent two days with Piet Oudolf, the Dutch garden designer and champion of our prairie flowers, traveling around Holland seeing gardens he designed, rich tapestries of perennials inevitably grown against a backdrop of green hedge. I noticed he never used variegated plants and asked him why. He shook his head in disdain, saying they were not natural-looking, too contrived, he felt, for the wild, meadowlike atmosphere he was often trying to achieve.

I think he was right. But I have always valued variegated perennials, shrubs, and even trees for the light and pattern they bring to a garden. Bosco, who is fond of decoration, the more ornate the better, has an indiscriminate weakness for these striped and splotched plants. If he sees one he doesn't own, he cannot resist bringing it home. We now have a burgeoning collection of spotted pulmonarias and brunneras. And heaven forbid he should see yet another new hosta that, splashed and dipped in yellow or white, strikes his fancy. Soon we will run out of shady spots for these fancy cabbages, unless we start putting them in our patch of woodland, where so far they have been banned, since we think, as Piet would, that they would appear unnatural there.

Variegation of leaf is probably not fitting where we are trying to achieve a wild-looking sort of garden, or copying a native landscape, but it is welcome in our garden beds. A large arching bush of the shrub dogwood, *Cornus alba* 'Elegantis-sima', decorates a corner of our white garden with its cream-tipped foliage above a carpet of a tiny-leaved, white-edged hosta named 'Louisa'. In the shrubbery just beyond the garden, our sapling *Cornus controversa* 'Variegata' will one day grow up to dazzle us with tiered branches of foliage rimmed and streaked with white. We have two different variegated daphnes in the terrace beds in front of the stone retaining walls. One is the well-known *D. burkwoodii* 'Carol Mackie', prettily dressed with whirls of narrow leaves edged in yellow, nestling pink-budded, scented white flowers in May. Even when not in flower, it is a handsome shrub because of its leaf pattern. The other is a hy-brid of the Caucasian daphne called *D.* × *transatlantica* 'Sum-mer Ice'. It has broader leaves, glossy green tongues dipped in cream, and its clusters of exquisitely perfumed four-petaled flowers linger through November.

The soft blue August flowers of the blue mist shrub (vari-eties of caryopteris) are its main attraction, but we have a charm-ing variegated sort called *C. divaricata* 'Snow Fairy' in the yellow garden. The shrub is pretty even when not in bloom. This October at Greenwood Gardens in New Jersey, I walked along an allée of pleached Japanese hornbeams underplanted with drifts of 'Snow Fairy', and it did not matter that it was no longer in bloom, thanks to the shimmer the light foliage gave to the scene.

Many ornamental grasses with streaks of white or yellow or red add valuable pattern and color to the garden. Here, creamy-edged *Molinia caerulea* 'Variegata' makes an attractive low clump by a path in the nasturtuim garden, mingling with peach dwarf bearded iris, and red-painted *Panicum virgatum* 'Shenandoah' offers two-to-three-foot verticals of deep color to accompany heucheras and cranesbills in the main garden. But my favorite is the Japanese forest grass, *Hakonechloa ma-*

cra 'Aureola', which brings imagined sunlight to the shadowy places it prefers. It is a low-growing grass, best seen toward the front of a bed or along the edge of a path, a graceful waterfall of golden-and-green-striped leaves with a telling visual effect. Several clumps lighten up the border beneath our black pussy willow in the yellow garden, contrasting with cranesbills, lungworts, and fat-leaved, yellow-variegated hostas there. A cream-and-green-striped sort, 'Albo-Striata', is slightly more upright in habit and nicely fills a corner of our white garden, appearing to tolerate more sun than its yellow-striped cousin.

Occasionally, our hybridists, in pursuit of the ever-different coloring and patterning of a leaf, come up with a plant that just looks diseased, but generally, variegated plants are irresistible eye candy. Because these decoratively streaked and spotted plants are so appealing to most of us gardeners, we risk having too many of them in the garden beds. Then they lose their effectiveness, merely creating a confusing busyness instead. It is better to use them as accents, features played against a dominant solid green field, or so I say gently to Bosco as he comes home with yet another variegated trophy.

DEATH ROW

When Bosco and I were first married, we drove up to Ithaca one May to visit our friend Hitch Lyman. Hitch lives in a handsome Greek Revival farmhouse that sits in a meadow surrounded by head-high bushes of old-time roses and lilacs and has a view of a folly in the perfect guise of a Doric temple. Hitch is a passionate and knowledgeable plantsman, and behind that temple he has an intricate garden of treasures brought home from his travels—delicate species peonies, rare snowdrops and colchicums, pink and white corydalis bred in Latvia, double hellebores, variegated burnets.

As we greeted Hitch outside his kitchen door, we couldn't help noticing to one side of the entrance a line of pots containing plants that were in various stages of decay—brittle stems, collapsed and browned leaves, rotted flowers. "What is that?" Bosco asked in barely contained horror. "That," said Hitch with a wave of his hand as he turned to lead us inside, "is Death Row."

Until I married Bosco, I too had a death row, though mine was hidden from view behind the compost area's fencing. There stood plants I had ordered in the dreamy enthusiasm of late winter, but hadn't got around to planting, and then forgot to water; plants given to me that I didn't really want and didn't know what to do with. Pathetically shriveled plants from which I averted my eyes as I dumped my wheelbarrow of weeds in the compost. The guilt was terrible, and, finally, when there was no hope of their survival, I would dump the plants out of their pots into the compost and quickly cover them, muttering apologies as though they could hear.

No longer. Bosco would never tolerate such waste. He was a European refugee, having gone as a child from plenty to very little, and now cherishes the belongings he has. And he is a nurturer. I still, now with Bosco as accomplice, order too many plants for the spring, come home with too many spur-of-the-moment purchases. But these are no longer allowed to languish. "Where do you want this dwarf vernonia to go?" he will ask me, and I have to stop and think in which border we can cram this autumn-blooming perennial that I couldn't resist. If I am too lazy or busy to do the planting right away, he marches off with a spade to sink the plant in himself.

My husband is equally queasy about throwing away our excess of perennials. Inevitably, we end up having too much of plants that colonize and creep by stolons beyond their allotted places. Others, like iris and summer phlox, we have in over-abundance after the periodic dividing and replanting they require. I used to think nothing of tossing the discards onto the compost heap. But not now that Bosco's around. He painstakingly pots them up, waters them in, then gives them away to willing friends or contributes them to our local library's plant sale. In the fall, I find a host of pots buried in the compost heap containing bits of plants he's quietly gathered and is storing until spring.

When Hitch comes to visit, he invariably brings us a choice plant he has dug up from his garden—one spring it was a tiny ruffled species daffodil, *Narcissus eystettensis*; another, a rare snowdrop, or, in autumn, a little fall-flowering allium, *A. thunbergii*. (In contrast, in the fullness of summer, he'll arrive with an armload of the gaudiest colored gladiolas—deliciously vulgar, he would say—or delphiniums in every shade of blue, from the farmers' market in Ithaca.) In return, Bosco gives him an heirloom tomato or a special variety of plectranthus or species geranium he's grown in the greenhouse, and I dig up a division of some perennial, like the white burnet, that he eyed in the garden. As Hitch drives away with these pots in the back of his Volvo, a quizzical expression flits across Bosco's face, and I know he is wondering if his plants will end up on Death Row.

NEW ARCHITECTURE

THE BOSCOTEL:
A ROOM OF HIS OWN

In the style of Vita Sackville-West and Harold Nicolson, Bosco and I have separate living quarters in which we spend at least part of our days. When we were married ten years ago, Bosco sold his stone gatehouse on the Hudson, a charming Victorian structure with high ceilings and tall arched windows, perfect for a man who had spent years of his adult life within the lofty and elegant confines of a Parisian apartment. He was ready for a new life, but perhaps not for the low-ceilinged, cozy, but admittedly inelegant New England–style farmhouse he moved into. Bosco complained that there was no room to hang pictures, most of the walls having been covered floor-to-ceiling with books. And he missed his high ceilings. So, with some of the money from the sale of his house, we built a small house of his own, not much more than a glorified room with a ten-foot-high coffered ceiling and a central fireplace. Inspired by a billboard advertising a sylvan hotel we saw once while traveling in Italy, we call it the Boscotel.

Designed by the Connecticut architect Peter Talbot to echo the simple Greek Revival details of the old farmhouse, it is a clapboard structure with wooden pilasters alternating with oversized windows along its south and west elevations. A glass-paned door leads into a small greenhouse on the east. The north side houses utilities, a bathroom, and a small office for Bosco's papers and computer. At first we had grand ideas of including

The Boscotel

a guest bedroom as well as a garden room and potting shed by the greenhouse. But the added cost discouraged us, and, perhaps even more important, we didn't want the scale of this outbuilding to overpower our small property and modest main house. In the spacious, sun-filled room of the Boscotel, an old sleigh bed is piled with cushions in one corner, small tables are scattered with bibelots and family photographs, and dark green wicker chairs and a sofa covered with palm-strewn chintz cluster around a fireplace. The high walls are hung with an ever-changing kaleidoscope of drawings and paintings. When he is not in the garden or away from home, this is where Bosco spends his daylight hours, writing, listening to opera, dozing after lunch, or working in the greenhouse. He comes down for meals.

The Boscotel is set on the highest knoll of our property, a place I used to call "May's hill" because my old Scottish deerhound, May, loved to lie there, with a full view of the comings and goings on the road and across the fields. Peter wisely persuaded us not to site the house in the middle or back of our property where the land is open and quite beautiful with views, but to set it to one side, near our boundary line, backing onto the graveled road to the barn. From here we would have a prospect of the best of our land.

The tall south windows of the house look down onto the gardens above the kitchen terrace, the glass-paned central door on axis with the path that runs through the small yellow garden into the herb garden beyond. The west windows face our new meadow on one side, the barn on the other, and, straight ahead, past an old sugar maple, the grass walk that leads to the vegetable garden and a picturesque view of the hills beyond our boundary stone wall. Tall French doors open out to a small gravel terrace here, edged in boxwood, and cluttered with cushioned wrought-iron chairs and an ever-changing collection of potted plants. This is our favorite place to sit on a summer evening with a chilled glass of rosé or champagne, watching the sun lower and set. The building of the Boscotel, and our use of its space, our coming to and fro, our lingering on its terrace, has provided a new experiencing of our land, celebrating a part of it that was virtually ignored by all but my old dog before Bosco came to Duck Hill.

THE GREENHOUSE

It is January, and I've just returned from a visit to the green-house, opening its door to a blessed smell of moist earth and fresh green. Outside, the ground is carpeted with snow, icicles drip off the gutters, all is shades of gray, taupe, and white. But inside this small magic world, geraniums bloom with abandon in pink and red, rosemaries are dusted with pale blue flowers, limes and calamondin oranges scent the air. South African lachenalias open candy-corn trumpets of red and yellow thrusting out at a forty-five-degree angle from crimson-mottled stalks above red-streaked leaves. Pots of freesias are in full pleated leaf, beginning to throw up slender budded stems that promise tiers of sweet flowers in white, lavender, and golden yellow. Snouts are emerging from the fleshy arching leaves of bold veltheimias.

On the center table, paperwhites (the less rankly perfumed sorts, like *Narcissus* 'Inbal') are in various stages of growth, wait-ing to be taken to the house as soon as blooms appear. Amaryllis are shooting up phallic budded stalks from bare earth, promis-ing extravagant lilylike flowers, pale-throated, striped, scarlet and white. A few tiny species narcissi that would not survive our cold outside are in grassy leaf, and I watch for signs of their miniature teardrop buds. We have not yet started to pull our pots of hardy daffodils, crocuses, scilla, and grape hyacinths out of the cold frame where they have been buried in shav-ings since October. But by the end of the month, we will be-gin to bring in a few at a time to wake up in the warmth of the greenhouse, to coax into bloom and then take down to the house.

This is Bosco's winter playground, and the staging place for all the plants that dress our tables from now until late spring, when the greenhouse bounty is upstaged by the profusion of flowering outdoors. But it is also where Bosco starts his seedlings for the vegetable garden sometime in late February and early March: first the leeks and onions, then the tomatoes and peppers that he will nurture until they can be transferred out of doors. Heirloom tomatoes are his specialty and he grows over two dozen sorts, sometimes pricking out as many as one hundred little plants to grow on and be shared with friends and sold at the library. He grows salvias too, from seed and cuttings, the Mexican sorts that would not survive our winters, as well as plectranthus with purple-backed leaves and deep lavender racemes. He fusses over varieties of citrus plants, hoping for fruit that he can turn into jam. He starts new begonias, inserting a leaf into perlite. He roots scented geraniums for our summer pots. In February he brings great tubs of agapanthus in from the garage and gives them water and fertilizer to wake them up. Lemon verbena is similarly brought back to life. By March not a bare inch of bench is to be seen beneath the masses of plants, young and old.

It is, mercifully, a small greenhouse, twelve feet wide by twenty feet long. It was fashioned for us by the craftsman Mark Ward from salvaged pieces of old greenhouses, which is his métier—in this case two "bays" of a 1930s Lord & Burnham structure from an estate in Massachusetts. The wood is the original cedar fitted around tempered glass. The metal "benches" that hold the plants are from another old greenhouse, and the wood and glass door from a third. Only the top shelves against the glass eaves are new, purchased at Home Depot. We love the idea that our greenhouse is recycled, that it has a history and is still in use.

Our only regret is that we didn't add that potting shed between the greenhouse and the Boscotel. A place to pot and store crockery and barrels of soil, with hooks for coats and room for boots and wide tables for working, is a much-craved-for luxury. As it is, Bosco pots in one cramped corner of the greenhouse, clay pots are stacked on the floor, and the barrels of potting soil, compost, and perlite crowd him as he works. Another large pail of "blue water" stands by the sink—a half-strength dilution of fertilizer in water that Bosco uses on his plants starting in February.

On the north side of the greenhouse, we have a graveled work area with cedar benches where Bosco can stand pots of plants in summer. Here agapanthus, eucomis, crocosmia, and gloriosa lilies are clustered until they begin to bloom. Two potted fig trees come to life and fruit here. Newly purchased plants are held on the benches until planted. Here too are our cold frames for forcing bulbs in winter and acclimating seedlings to the outdoors after the warmth of the greenhouse in spring. A hedge of the gray-twigged dogwood, *Cornus racemosa*, divides the work area from the barn road. The door of the greenhouse opens east onto our mini-meadow and apple trees, and on the south side, a hedge of double pink-flowering burnet roses stands against its whitewashed brick foundation.

We keep the minimum temperature at forty-five degrees in the interest of conserving on our heating bill, but on a sunny day the greenhouse toasts up quickly. One automatic vent in the glass keeps the heat moderated, and other vents can be opened by hand. By mid-May, when young plants can easily sizzle in the heat, the glass is sprayed with a sheer white greenhouse paint for some relief from the sun. Nonetheless, coats and sweaters are thrown off in the moist warmth, and a straw hat is kept handy to shade Bosco's head as he pots and pricks out and waters. Arias from an opera recording waft from his house. Bosco is a happy man.

THE POOL

I learned years ago, from the talented garden designers I met and wrote about, how important water is in a garden: its sound, its reflections, the shimmering, mirrorlike light it brings to a landscape. We have no stream or pond at Duck Hill, set as we are high on the side of a valley. A few stone troughs of water attract iridescent dragonflies and provide drinks for the birds and dogs. But I wanted a larger water feature in the garden. And Bosco longed for a pool. Swimming is his favorite form of exercise besides the slow aerobics of gardening. We decided to build one in the old paddock beyond the garden, some distance from the house, in full sun, with a borrowed view of fields and distant hills beyond our western boundary. Although it was to be primarily for swimming, I was determined to have it be a pleasure to see in the landscape.

A long, narrow pool, in essence a lap pool, fifty feet long, seemed ideal. At first I wanted it only ten feet wide, but, wisely, Bosco persuaded me to make it wide enough for children to safely run and leap and dive. We settled on fifty feet by fourteen. Steps run the width of the shallow end, ideal for sitting on a sizzling summer day, ankles cooling, or for harboring toddler grandchildren. I sited the pool so that the length of it was on axis with the center of our yellow garden, just below the Boscotel, as well as the gate at the far west end of our property that leads out to a sixteen-acre field. The land in the paddock slopes gently to the south, as it does almost everywhere on our property, and so the ground where the pool was to be set needed leveling. We cut into the slope just north of its long side and had a three-foot-high dry retaining wall built with local granite stones. At the foot of the wall, an arbor, thirty feet long and ten feet wide, was constructed with posts from black locust trees, some of which were felled when we built the Boscotel. I was careful to design the arbor high enough—ten feet—so that shade seekers would not have to duck beneath its rose-draped timbers. Beneath the arbor, flat fieldstones were set in gravel for a terrace, and here I planted creeping thymes to fill in the cracks. The vigorous white rambler 'Seagull' was planted to climb the north side of the arbor and spill across its top, quickly providing the shade we wanted here.

We painted the concrete base of the pool a French gray, which subtly colors the water a natural sky blue. A flat stone edging around the pool meets a wide strip of lawn, which extends to the meadow beyond. The high grass and flowers of the meadow, as I had hoped, serve as a lively screen, giving the pool a sense of seclusion and privacy, at the same time visually connecting to the fields beyond our boundary. The split rail fence that originally surrounded the paddock, and now contains the meadow and pool, is clothed with stiff green plastic-coated wire, a safety measure required by law. The wire, we found to our delight, made a perfect surface for clematis to climb, and, gradually, we planted a collection of them along its length, favoring the wilder, more delicate texensis and viticella hybrids that flower in summer. Rosebushes also spill over the fence—the lovely white 'City of York', double blush 'Baltimore Belle', the pink prairie rose (*Rosa setigera*), and the apple rose (*R. pomifera*), with crab-apple-like hips in September.

Pool equipment—the unsightly, humming pump, heater, and filters—is always a challenge to hide. We sited it at the very bottom of the meadow's slope, out of earshot, against the fence.

We then hid the equipment from view by building a wall of stacked firewood around it, leaving a small gap to reach the pool workings. It was a cheap and instant solution to the problem of concealment, for we had an excess of wood from some dead ash trees that needed felling. And it seemed more fitting to the rustic site than latticework or stodgy evergreens.

The pool, not surprisingly, is a lure for visiting children and grandchildren, a joy for Bosco, and, even more than I hoped, a luminous water feature—at least for the six months, from May through October, when it is not covered with a dark green tarp. If you stand in the yellow garden at its cross axis, your eye is now drawn past sunflowers and beds of daylilies, past the wooden gate leading into the paddock, to the long shimmering pool. Surrounded by high grass and distant trees, the water mirrors the sky, reflects the sunlight, celebrates the space.

THE CHICKEN HOUSE

In the last ten years, the rash of building we've done at Duck Hill has substantially influenced the development of the garden. New architecture dictates new patterns and perspectives outdoors, and I've continued to play on the straight lines and long views suggested by architectural structures, finding in their sequential orderliness a certain deep satisfaction. Only the wilder parts of our property, such as the little woodland and the even smaller apple orchard, seem to call for sinuous paths and waving borders. The rest of the garden is linked, its disparate parts held together, by a series of linear backbones. And so the long narrow pool becomes the central feature in an axial view that runs from the yellow garden to the distant hills. The south front of the Boscotel ends the perspective from the series of patterned gardens below it. And the new chicken house is the destination of the long central path through the refurbished vegetable garden, its folly and its glory.

Chickens have always been part of the scenery at Duck Hill. At first we had no separate quarters for them, and they roosted at night in the barn, on a bar across one of the stalls, squeezed snugly next to one another in a row—except for one small bantam hen who insisted on roosting on the rump of our old hunter, a part-Clydesdale gentle giant who didn't seem to mind the company. But on warm summer nights, with the stalls' Dutch doors wide open, we found we were inviting raccoons to come

The chicken house

in for a slaughter. A lean-to shed on the back of the barn was quickly built to house the fowl, which included ducks and geese as well as chickens; and, finally, a freestanding house was thrown up beyond the barn, a thoroughly disreputable-looking but serviceable structure, mercifully smothered by 'Seagull' and 'Seven Sisters' roses every June.

When Bosco and I were married, we refashioned the barn, now empty of creatures, into a small apartment and a one-car garage that has never seen a car but is a handy place to store garden furniture and dormant agapanthus and figs. The apartment has French doors that open out to our western view, where in the foreground the unsightly henhouse stood. It had to go. I asked our friend Hitch, who has a love of classical architecture, to design us a new building that would comfortably house the chickens and, at the same time, be an architectural folly in the Greek Revival spirit of our farmhouse and the Boscotel. Classical chicken coops were not uncommon in the early nineteenth century, and examples can still be found, especially in England and France.

Hitch drew us up a temple, albeit a tiny one, a Doric conceit in clapboard, thirteen feet in length by seven deep, with a paneled doorway framed by rounded, fluted pilasters. Two flat pilasters, similar to the ones on the front of our farmhouse, decorate the corners of the coop. Its steep shingled roof has flourishes on either end, little curlicues of wood called anthemia. The eaves on the sides are pierced in a crisscross pattern for ventilation, and unseen windows open on the back for more air and light. My oldest son, Keith, with an archaeological doctorate under his belt, announced that our new chicken house looked like a mausoleum. In fact, it is not lugubrious at all, but silly, fanciful, and full of life.

It was built by a skilled carpenter, a friend of ours and Hitch's, in Ithaca, New York, and brought down in pieces in a van, then erected a short distance west of the barn apartment. It faces south, its back to the woods, at the far end of what became the central axis of the enclosed vegetable garden. You see it first as you come around the barn, beyond the clematis-draped fence, a creamy white folly backed by tall trees, in the summer framed by the yellow daisies of silphium and sunflowers and the conical plumes of hydrangeas. Two steps lead down from the doorway into the garden and, on either side, we planted peonies—the early delicate single white 'Windflower' (my favorite) and blush-pink 'Lady Gay'. Spring-blooming creeping *Veronica pedunculosa* 'Georgia Blue', with tiny, sparkling true-blue four-petaled flowers and dark green leaves flushed on their backsides with maroon, spills out into the path from the steps. The split rail fence that encloses the vegetable garden is attached to the chicken coop at the two corners of its front facade. On the sides of the house, beyond the fencing, small doors and ramps allow its residents easy access into a chicken run that extends around two sides of the vegetable garden. The front door of the temple opens into a narrow room where feed bins stand. On each side, a secondary door leads into a nesting and roosting area, and flaps open on hinges along the rest of the side walls so you can collect eggs from the nesting boxes without going into the inevitably grotty chicken bedrooms.

At first we had some banties among our brood—the fetching miniatures in the chicken world. They are less domesticated than most hens, and small enough to easily fly, and, to our dismay, they loved landing in the vegetable garden to feast on lettuces and fruit. Even worse, undetected by us, one diminutive hen decided to sit on a nest of eggs within the garden, safely hidden under the great paddle-shaped leaves of rhubarb. Twenty-one days later, we found our vegetable garden overrun with adorable, cheeping, fuzzy yellow, voracious chicks that would retreat under their mother's wing at our approach. Netting has since been added above the split rail fence to discourage such landings. And we've sadly given up on bantams and now stick to the heavier breeds of chickens that aren't so adept at flying.

The proximity of the chicken house to the vegetable garden offers more amusement than head-shaking. I enjoy being serenaded by clucking and crowing as I weed the beds, hearing announcements of a bug found or an egg laid. My baskets of weeds, bolted lettuce, mushy tomatoes, or submarine-sized zucchini are welcomed with a flurry of excitement. The house itself, this lively, egg-laden architectural hennery, seems an apt centerpiece of our pleasurably productive garden.

MULTISEASONAL
PLANTS

DOGWOODS

The longer I garden and the older I get, the more I appreciate plants that offer interest in more than one season. It is easy enough to have beauty in May and June, but how does the foliage stand up in summer? Is there fall color? Fruit? Nice seed heads? Is the shape of the plant pleasing, the bark decorative? The woody members of the dogwood family win a first prize on all accounts. Whether small trees or shrubs, they have handsome leaves, flowers, and fruit, a graceful branching habit, and often patterned or stunningly colored bark.

The beautiful eastern flowering dogwood, *Cornus florida*, appeared in lavish numbers where I grew up outside Philadelphia, gracing suburban gardens as well as large parks and country properties. I walked a mile to school every day along a well-traveled road where no sidewalks protected me from the rush of traffic, and I have mostly miserable memories of that walk in my crisply ironed cotton uniform and laced-up cream-colored bucks, dodging dust and mud thrown by passing cars. As the young leaves unfurled on the trees in early spring, I would arrive at school delicately pulling inchworms out of my hair, hoping no one would notice. But for a moment in May, all indignities were forgiven as I walked in a snow flurry of white and pink from the dogwoods that swept the road and laced overhead.

Before moving to Duck Hill, I lived with my family just south of here on an eighteen-acre property of open field and woods. Dogwoods littered the understory of our oak and tulip woodland and wept out onto the edges of the large meadow. Just before we left in 1981, the fungus anthracnose began killing dogwoods everywhere in our region, and I watched those lovely trees decline and begin to die. In the aftermath of that devastation, we were advised not to plant our native *C. florida*, but to choose the Asian *C. kousa* instead, for it appeared able to withstand the disease. Many crosses between our native *C. florida* and the kousa dogwood were developed as a compromise. But I was never willing to give up on this favorite tree, trusting, hoping it would overcome its period of plague. Fortunately, our flowering dogwood appears to be rallying. Now it is being used again in front yards, and I spot young saplings sprouting up on their own in the rough fields around here.

We have planted thirteen small trees of *C. florida* at Duck Hill, choosing a tried-and-true white-flowering variety called 'Cherokee Princess' that has shown resistance to anthracnose. Thirteen is not nearly enough. Bosco would like a very pale pink sort, and I want to plant at least five more white ones to drift through our little wood. *C. florida* is to me the most elegant of all our native understory trees, and even in youth adds beauty to the garden. Its ovate leaves are dark green and handsomely ribbed. In May the showy flower display slowly develops over a period of weeks. Four petal-like bracts, at first creamy white tinged with green, unfurl around the actual green flower head, and gradually age to a dazzling pure white, each bract notched with a dab of rose pink. They are followed by clusters of glossy red berries, which the birds quickly consume in early autumn when the foliage deepens to a striking purply red. In winter the trees are lovely because of their picturesque branching, each upturned twig topped with a round nubby bud. As they age, the trees spread horizontally, becoming as wide as they are high.

Although it does not have quite the delicacy or grace of our native *C. florida*, *C. kousa* is a splendid tree to have in the garden. It is stouter, less wild-looking, statuesque, and very showy. It flowers later than our native dogwood, in June, and is littered then with tiers of white bracts followed by raspberry-like fruits in the fall. With maturity, the trunks of kousas exfoliate and develop a gorgeous mottling of gray, brown, and beige. I was sent a small cutting of this dogwood about twenty years ago—it came in the mail from the Brooklyn Botanic Garden as a membership bonus—and it now towers to thirty feet by the west side of the barn, spreading its flowered and fruited branches beneath the property's boundary of maples.

One spring a few years ago, as Bosco and I were prowling around our favorite woody nursery nearby, I caught sight of a dogwood with huge glistening white bracts. We succumbed to impulse buying, as we often do, egged on by each other, and brought it home. It is called 'Venus' and is a hybrid resulting from a cross first between *C. kousa* and *C. florida* and then with the native Pacific dogwood, *C. nuttallii*, introduced to the trade by Rutgers University. It is said to grow rapidly and has lustrous green leaves and flowers (bracts, really) the size of butter plates. We have planted it at the end of the white garden where we lost the old white ash, and I watch it with fondness as one of my indulgences.

C. alternifolia is an underappreciated native dogwood that naturalizes in our patch of woods at Duck Hill. As its name suggests, it is the only member of the family with alternating, rather than opposite, leaves. Also aptly called the pagoda dogwood, it is an incredibly graceful small tree with a layered pattern of horizontal, spreading branches, ideally suited to the wooded understory where it relieves the vertical thrust of the great hardwood trees. It flowers in late spring, thankfully just after its more glamorous cousin *C. florida*, and the show is quiet but effective, the tiered branches dusted with flat-topped cymes of soft cream-colored flowers. The flowers are followed by drupes that change from green to pink to blue-black in late summer. A selection of *C. alternifolia* called 'Argentea' is prettily variegated in leaf, white and pink.

C. controversa is the Asian version of our *C. alternifolia*, and its variety 'Variegata' is in maturity the most stunningly beautiful variegated tree I know. With delicate tiers of creamy-white-edged leaves, the little tree lights up a landscape as if it were in flower. It is another of our indulgences. Bosco and I brought home a tiny sapling of this dogwood three years ago and planted it at the beginning of our small wood, in close proximity to the white garden. Last winter, a deer broke into our garden and, to our horror, ate all the young branches down to the main stem. We replaced the dogwood with a new specimen, a gift from a friend, and this time wrapped chicken wire around it. I watch it lovingly, hoping that we will live long enough to see it put on a show. It is said to grow more rapidly and be sturdier than the variegated *C. alternifolia*.

I am quite fond of a very different dogwood, *Cornus mas*, commonly and confusingly known as the cornelian cherry. You notice it along the old parkways going into New York when it is in flower in March, covered with umbels of little gold threads. Besides the splendid hedge of this dogwood around our parking area, we have one old specimen of it farther along the barn road near our cold frames, about twenty feet high, multistemmed but treelike in stature, with pale gray bark. It is a fresh blaze of warm spring color when most of the garden is still gray and cold. It has the handsome dark-green ribbed leaves typical of dogwoods, and in July, fruit develops in the shape of oval drupes, ripening slowly from green to deep red. Bosco painstakingly collects the fruit when it is fully ripe and makes a deliciously tart jam.

Shrub dogwoods can be stellar additions to garden borders as well as the wilder garden near woodland. We grow several sorts at Duck Hill. The Tartarian dogwood in its variegated form, *C. alba* 'Elegantissima', enlivens a corner of our white garden in every season. The many stems, rising to six feet, are crimson and particularly telling in the winter landscape, especially in snow. The stems become secondary when the shrub leafs out, for the green leaves are margined generously with creamy white, lightening up what is a somewhat shadowy corner in this small garden. In June flat cymes of fuzzy white flowers appear, not remarkable in themselves but softly effective. Bosco cuts out one or two branches of the oldest growth down to the ground every spring in order to encourage new shoots, which will be the brightest red. But we are careful not to take away the grace of the bush, which arches decoratively over the low boxwood hedge that frames this garden.

'Bud's Yellow' is a variety of *C. alba* with chartreuse stems that we have planted in a bed of the main garden where the soil is rather moist and it is sunny only part of the day. It too is a pleasure to see in winter when vibrant color is at a premium. Last spring we planted several bushes of the vivid apricot-stemmed dogwood called 'Cato' in the shrubbery along our southern boundary. It is a cultivar of the European bloodtwig dogwood, *C. sanguinea*, more compact than the better-known 'Midwinter Flame', which is said to sucker and grow rankly. In any case, copsing, or cutting back hard, encourages young growth and the most vivid coloring.

My favorite shrub dogwood, *C. racemosa*, proliferates at the edge of the old fields around Duck Hill, forming graceful swelling colonies that please the eye throughout the year. The gray or panicled dogwood, as it is called, has the ribbed ovate leaves and dusty white flowers typical of all the shrubby sorts. But in late summer, it develops small round chalk-white berries that are held upright on delicate pinkish red stalks, or pedicels. After the fruit is eaten by birds, the stalks persist, giving the bushes a lovely rosy blush, even in winter. In autumn the foliage of the gray dogwood deepens to a burnished maroon, a stunning foil for the golds and butter yellows of the season. We have planted a few bushes at the western edge of our property, hoping they will naturalize, but they are struggling in the shade of some sugar maples there. Three years ago, I planted a hedge of the gray dogwood stretching from the barn to the Boscotel, to conceal the road and any cars parked up at the barn from where we like to sit in summer evenings on the terrace by Bosco's house. I've never heard of this dogwood being used in this way, but, in fact, it makes a lovely, informal four-foot hedge, and I trust that I can contain its suckering proclivities by the gravel drive on one side and the mowed lawn on the other. It is an experiment, and already I wonder if I have allowed enough room for its natural curvaceous shape.

In early September last year, caterpillars as white as the bushes' berries appeared en masse, hiding curled beneath the leaves, and worked their dogged way through the foliage until our hedge was prematurely bare. Next year we'll watch it like a hawk and, if the caterpillars start to hatch, we'll spray the leaves with the environmentally acceptable BT (*Bacillus thuringiensis*). Alternatively, we could knock them off into a can of soapy water, a satisfying occupation, or import a flock of guinea hens.

VIBURNUMS

There's a viburnum beetle on the loose, *Pyrrhalta viburni* by name, and if its taste in the species turns out to be indiscriminate, we are in trouble. Over the years, I've planted just about every viburnum I could get my hands on. This tribe of plants is loved as much—in my case even more—for its fruit as for its flowers. The vibrant fruit is red, black, or blue, sometimes all three in succession, occasionally yellow, and is held in clusters that are showy in late summer, autumn, and often through early winter. Most of the fruiting viburnums, I find, want some good hours of sun for the best display of berries. Some benefit from being planted in multiples. I was astonished recently to see *V. dilatatum* 'Michael Dodge', at a friend's house, massed against a sunny wall. This cultivar is coveted for its unusual canary yellow fruit, but our one bush of 'Michael Dodge', growing in the dappled shade of our woods, is bereft of berries, whereas my friend's bushes were laden. I think we need to plant another clone or two, in a sunnier spot.

The foliage of many viburnums, whether they are grown for their fruit or their flowers, remains healthy through our humid summers, so these are worthy shrubs for our yards. In autumn, a number of them color up nicely in shades of red, orange, russet, and mahogany.

Which are my favorites? For berries, the tea viburnum, *V. setigerum*, gets my top vote. It is a willowy, narrow-growing

Viburnum trilobum
fruit

multistemmed shrub, the smooth gray trunks about seven feet tall and arching, especially with the weight of its fruit, which develops in late summer and drips in clusters from every small branch. The inch-long drupes are oval in shape, glossy Christmas red, and hang by the dozens from delicate stems beneath large, narrow leaves of deep green. Plant this shrub in groupings of three at least, if you have the room. The tea viburnum does well in an open spot in our woodland where it gets two, perhaps three, hours of sun.

The linden viburnum, *V. dilatatum* 'Erie', is another favorite for its fruiting. It is stout in habit, densely covered with lustrous, heavily ribbed leaves, a lush and fulsome shrub to about eight feet. In October our three bushes, which line a length of our driveway, are covered with sprays of tiny deep red fruit, giving the appearance from a distance of a haze of red. The leaves of this viburnum stay green until they fall, but the fruit remains on the bare-twigged shrubs through most of winter.

By late October, our native cranberry bush, *V. trilobum*, is ratty in leaf, brown-tinged and ragged-edged, and it is a happy day when the leaves are shed. But for late autumn and early winter display, the fruit of this medium-sized, loosely twiggy shrub is as showy as any. The berries are fat and squooshy, translucent, glistening, bright scarlet, hanging from gray branches in generous clusters. They are beautiful to see against an early snowfall. Last January a flock of cedar waxwings, feathered gray-brown with jaunty berets and mascara-streaked eyes, came to dine on the berries.

On our kitchen terrace, we have a six-foot bush of the well-known Koreanspice viburnum, *V. carlesii*, which is arguably the most fragrant of all this clan, and it certainly smells delicious when it flowers in May. But its coarse leaves curl and become misshapen soon after its rounded flowers fade (I believe due to a bug), and its stiff, upright habit can appear awkward. Fall coloring is nonexistent. For similarly fragrant flowers, *V. × burkwoodii* is my preferred choice because of its graceful habit and richly painted fall foliage. Our bushes of the Burkwood viburnum, at the south corners of the house, are considerably taller, to ten feet, and pleasantly vase-shaped, the branches arching with their pom-pom flowers in May, tinged at first with dusky pink, then fading to white, their spicy sweetness thrown into the air. The small, oblong leaves are healthy all summer and in October become prettily speckled with red and yellow.

We have two other viburnums with pom-pom flowers that are among my favorites, one called 'Popcorn', the other 'Mary Milton'. They are both new cultivars of the Japanese snowball viburnum, *V. plicatum*, which is prized not for fragrance but for its elegant way of growing in horizontal tiers. 'Popcorn' has fat, round white flowers, like popcorn balls at an amusement park, that litter the outstretched branches. Its flowering is outrageously, unabashedly showy, with something of the clown about it. By October the deeply ribbed and wrinkled ovate leaves have abandoned their rich deep green for a red mahogany.

When I first saw *V.* 'Mary Milton' in flower in a pot, I nearly swooned, I thought it was so pretty. What is it about certain plants that causes us to turn into jelly? Of course, I had to have one. The pom-pom flowers are what I can only describe as old-lady pink, not the childlike pink of bubble gum but the soft, pale rose hue of faded aprons and caked face powder. The leaves are broad and matte in sheen, dark green when mature, but felty and tinged with bronze when young, nicely setting off the flowers. We now have a small specimen of 'Mary' at Duck Hill, and I wait impatiently for it to grow up. I want the day to come when it is a presence in the landscape and I can cut an armload of its blooming branches for a vase indoors.

The leaves of some of our arrowwoods this autumn are punctured with small holes, telltale signs of the leaf beetle, and the undersides of the twigs are dotted with dark bumps all in a row, caps the beetles excrete to neatly enclose their eggs in pinhole cavities. According to studies, this native species (*V. dentatum*), which proliferates in the woodland at Duck Hill, and *V. sargentii* are the beetles' favorites. Apparently they don't sniff at two other shade-tolerant natives we grow and admire— *V. acerifolium*, the maple-leaf viburnum, and the black haw, *V. prunifolium*. So far ours seem healthy enough. To combat the beetle, we are told to prune out and throw away any infested twigs in the winter, when the egg sites are easiest to spot. The beetles themselves can be knocked into tubs of sudsy water, like the rose-loving Japanese beetle when it's groggy in the morning and at dusk—a task worth doing for the many-season beauty of these shrubs.

WITCH HAZELS

I remember as a child having witch hazel rubbed on me by my parents to soothe an itchy leg or sunburned back, but it wasn't until I was riding a horse in some damp woods here in North Salem, merely fifteen or twenty years ago, that I finally came face-to-face with the native shrub from which this mild astringent is extracted. It was November, and all the trees but oaks were bare, and suddenly ahead of me I saw a willowy shrub that was washed all over with yellow. I thought at first leaves were making that color, but no, they were flowers, yellow, spidery-petaled flowers up and down the stems. *Hamamelis virginiana* is a common understory shrub in these parts, rarely noticed in bloom, though the wavy-edged golden autumn leaves are handsome in themselves. American Indians were the first to value the bark and leaves of this shrub, brewed as a tea for colds and as an astringent for sore muscles and used as a poultice for inflammations. We learned recently from the Connecticut plantsman Adam Wheeler that the first witch hazel distillery was started in Essex, Connecticut, just north of here, in 1866, to produce the revered liniment that my parents used.

Some years ago, we planted this fall-blooming common witch hazel, as it is called, at the west end of our woodland walk, where it catches some morning sun. It was a small rooted cutting when we received it from a mail-order nursery; it grew slowly to six feet but refused to bloom. I was beginning to despair when, finally, the small yellow threads made their debut last autumn. Eventually it should reach a tree height of twenty or thirty feet. This past spring, we bought a young bush less than two feet high of a compact form called 'Little Suzy' and planted it in a lightly shaded spot nearby where two paths converge. Walking by on a gray day this November, I happened to notice, to my delight and astonishment, that this baby shrub was already decorated with fragrant golden tassels.

Hamamelis virginiana is the only species of witch hazel that blooms in the fall. All the rest are early spring bloomers, so early in fact that it is fair to say they are really late winter performers, often opening their brightly colored threads by the middle of February. *H. vernalis*, which is native to a small area of the Ozarks, is always the first to flower here, small burnished orange and yellow threads, clustered around a red calyx, that usually have a sweet fruity fragrance. Having said that, I should add that we have one handsome stand of the spring witch hazel halfway along the woodland path that some years emits a musty smell at best, and another bush at the entrance to the wood that is reliably and intensely fragrant. On bitter cold days, the little spidery flowers roll up tight, opening again with any hint of sun and warmth. *H. vernalis* grows in an upright fashion on silvery gray trunks. It is the only witch hazel that suckers, creating a thicket in time.

The showiest witch hazels are cultivars of the Chinese species *H. mollis* and hybrid crosses of *H. mollis* and *H. japonica*, known as *H. × intermedia*. These offer larger flowers in every variation from yellow to orange to red, often with excellent fragrance and a picturesque spreading habit of growth. We grow one cultivar of the Chinese species at the edge of our wooded area, the bright yellow upright-growing 'Sweet Sunshine', which throws its sweet scent into the air. The equally fragrant *H. × intermedia* hybrid 'Pallida' stretches its elegant limbs on the south side of our driveway beneath some maples, greeting us all of March with its pale sulfur-yellow threads, which curl around deep red calyxes. To one side of it, we planted the selection 'Diane' as a contrast, with deep orange-red crimped tassels. The leaves of 'Pallida' turn a beautiful golden yellow in the autumn, and those of 'Diane' deepen to a rich red. Recently, on a whim, we brought home a showy hybrid called 'Harry' for a half-sunny spot along our wooded path. It boasts huge brassy golden yellow flowers that will cheer us at the beginning of spring.

Witch hazels are virtually disease-free, only requiring a humus-rich, moderately acid soil in high-canopy shade or full sun. They are all-season shrubs—their leaves are handsome, ribbed, broadly oval, and remain healthy throughout the summer, turning a burnished gold or red in fall. In early winter, the branches are promisingly studded with fat buds.

The only drawback of this family of plants is that they are excruciatingly slow to grow up. Unless you buy trophy-sized specimens to begin with, you'll have to have some patience and hang around in one garden long enough, as I have, to see them mature. I planted our bush of 'Pallida' fifteen years ago and it is just now starting to relax its vase shape and spread its limbs. Witch hazels eventually expand into a picturesque gracefulness, their interlacing twigs fanning out in a horizontal manner.

If you can go to see a collection of mature witch hazels in an arboretum or botanical garden when they are in flower, it is worth the trouble. They are an astonishing sight in the leafless days of late winter, eating the ground with their fanned branches dusted yellow and gold and Pompeiian red, breathtaking seen against a background of evergreens.

AUTUMN THEATRICS

In a northeast autumn, subtlety is abandoned as nature shows us finally and emphatically that all colors go together—a notion we gardeners sometimes resist. Shocking pink and orange, clear yellow and vermilion, winey, purply red with the most strident gold, chestnut, and magenta, play against the greens of conifers, lawn, and field, and, typically, a deep cerulean sky. It seems every color is present in this tapestry with the exception of hard china white. The whites, even of roses and chrysanthemums, are soft now, cream, buff-edged, rose-tinged. During this season, in October and November, flowers take on a secondary role, rather like small unexpected bonuses, and the glorious color of foliage moves to center stage in the garden as well as in the landscape.

Beneath the old sugar maples at Duck Hill, blazing golden orange in mid-October, the rich burgundy red leaves of the flowering dogwoods are a counterpoint to the sunlit yellows of spicebush (*Lindera benzoin*) at the property's edge and summersweet (*Clethra alnifolia*), which colonizes in our wood. Clethra is slow to leaf out in the spring and remains quietly green all summer. It saves its star performance for late in the season, surprising us in August with white, fuzzy, upright racemes that are intensely perfumed and humming with bees. A number of selections are on the market with lovely pink spikes, among them the charming deep pink 'Ruby Spice'. Summersweet is, like spicebush, a local native, growing wild in deep wet woodlands here, where it rises to impressive heights of ten feet or more and throws its delicious scent into the moist air when it flowers. Even at Duck Hill, where the ground is invariably dry in summer, generous clumps flourish and perfume our shadowy woodland walk. In October the bushes offer an encore with their glowing butter-yellow foliage.

Surrounding the front courtyard, the dwarf winged euonymus hedge (*E. alatus* 'Compactus'), hardly dwarf at six feet and wanting to be even taller, screams in its shocking pink dress. The dwarf Korean lilacs enclosing the herb garden are a more muted but pleasing coppery hue, and the low-growing blueberry bushes that circle the center bed of this garden are brilliant crimson. In the flower gardens, *Geranium macrorrhizum*, the scented cranesbill that makes such a splendid ground cover, is streaked and edged cherry red. Clumps of amsonia are transformed from fresh green to warm yellow, and the ornamental grasses—pennisetums, descampsias, molinias, panicums, and hakonechloas—are their most provocative, with waving streamers and tassels of golden beige.

It is a soft, sunlit day in early November as I write this, and the hills out my windows are muted after the fireworks of October, now painted lilac gray and dotted with the rust brown of oaks, alone in still clinging to their leaves. The sugar maples, ashes, hickories, black cherries, and locusts are bare-branched. Only scattered leaves pooling the ground—amber, carmine, apricot, russet—hint at their past brilliance. In the garden, however, vignettes of vivid foliage remain to thrill my eye.

At the edge of the woodland path, a grove of eight-foot-high fothergilla (*F. major*), plain green and virtually unnoticed all summer, has colored shades of pumpkin orange. Flanking the fothergilla are oakleaf hydrangeas, their large wrinkled leaves an inky maroon sometimes flashed with scarlet, providing a handsome foil. Low bushes of sweetspire (*Itea virginica* 'Henry's Garnet') arch gracefully nearby, with elliptic leaves of brilliant crimson. The foliage of itea holds on into December and branches are as beautiful cut for tall vases indoors as they are in the garden. A native of the pine barrens of New Jersey and farther south, sweetspire will naturalize in a moist part of the garden, though it has yet to do that here. In spring its branches are tipped with fragrant white racemes of flowers.

Fothergilla also has a show of fragrant flowers in May, odd white bottlebrushes, smelling of licorice, but its most vivid moment is when it colors up in the fall. The dwarf fothergilla, *F. gardenii*, that I bought and planted in a cluster beneath my dressing room window many years ago is said to be a smaller plant altogether, maturing at three feet, but mine is now six feet tall, blocking much of the light with its slender, wavy branches and rounded, scalloped leaves. This is not at all what I had in mind (I suspect it was mislabeled and is, in fact, a hybrid between *F. gardenii* and *F. major*) and I am in a quandary as to what to do about it. If I shear the bushes back, I will destroy their willowy grace, and if I remove old wood at the base, I'll still have young branches shooting to six feet and screening my window. I think I will leave it be and enjoy its pretty, irregular branching and spectacular fall foliage up close. In autumn, when the leaves are ablaze with orange, gold, and scarlet, they tint and warm the interior walls and window seat where I dress. The fothergillas are members of the witch hazel family, indigenous to mountains and coastal plains from Virginia to South Carolina, but are perfectly hardy here and appear to thrive in our moderately acid soil.

The oakleaf hydrangea, *H. quercifolia*, is also a native in more southern states, and it sometimes dies back to the ground in very cold winters for us. But it rises again and, though it blooms mostly on stems produced in the previous season, it will flower also on new wood. The handsome form 'Snowflake', with extra sepals that give it a lush, double-flowered appearance, is thought to be hardier than some other named cultivars. In summer this hydrangea's huge panicles of flowers change from white to wine pink to buff. I love it now in its rich purple dress, with soft brown plumes hanging on. All three of these native shrubs are gems to plant in partially shaded parts of the garden.

On the east side of the house, the camellia-flowered stewartia has for weeks now been a spectacular burnt orange. And just to one side of it, a tall arching *Viburnum* × *burkwoodii* hangs on to its small green leaves, speckled and splashed with yellow, tangerine, and scarlet. You don't have to be outdoors to savor this fiery display, for the stewartia and viburnum are just beyond our living room windows, and their dazzling color becomes part of the room's decoration as you pass by or linger there. From almost anywhere on the property or from our west-facing upstairs windows, you catch glimpses of the purple-leaved smokebush, *Cotinus coggygria* 'Royal Purple', which, in autumn, is a showstopper below the Boscotel. The leaves are a dazzling kaleidoscope of colors, deep ruby red with flashes of orange and vermilion. We pollard this large bush every March, cutting the waving stems back to nubbins on the old twisting branches that rise about six feet. In summer, the newly grown stems of beautiful paddle-shaped leaves are a lively, almost translucent purply maroon.

Two years ago, we were given a small specimen of *Cotinus obovatus*, the American smoketree, by a friend, and planted it in a spot of sunshine along the barn road. I immediately went to the books to read all about it, for this native plant was unfamiliar to me, growing naturally in only a few select places like the mountains of Tennessee and Alabama. It is prized by those who know it for its spectacular show in autumn when grown in at least four or five hours of sun. Bill Cullina writes that the large oval leaves begin to glow then, "as if lit from within." Our little tree already gives us hints of the autumnal brilliance we can expect over the years. The leaves are held up like Asian fans by bright red petioles that continue up their centers, their green slowly flushing to flame colors. Some are streaked with orange, others golden-flushed; others still have edges dipped in wine.

WINTER BARK, BUDS, AND PODS

The flowering of magnolias, as ravishing as it is, lasts a week if we're lucky enough not to have a late spring frost that turns the large, elegantly beautiful waxy flowers brown. But these singular trees are nevertheless excellent examples of multiseason beauty, for they have a picturesque habit of growth with branches sinuously interlacing, their bark is a beautiful silvery gray, and in winter the trees are tipped all over with long fur-coated buds.

We have four magnolias at Duck Hill, certainly all our congested acreage can accommodate. *Magnolia stellata*, the star magnolia, is a beloved player here, and, because of its moderate height (to about twenty feet), is a good choice for the smaller garden. It is a rounded, shrublike tree with the smooth pale gray bark typical of the family and buds reminiscent of a willow's catkins on the tips of every twig. The green-tinged furry winter buds split open on a warm day in April to reveal strappy satin-white flowers, actually tepals, tinged with pink as they age. Our star magnolia is sheltered against the west side of our bedroom wing, where it is somewhat protected from the morning sun and therefore less apt to be burned by a wayward late frost. In bloom it throws off a soft fragrance, best appreciated up close.

A taller, more statuesque hybrid, *Magnolia × loebneri* 'Merrill', which was developed at the Arnold Arboretum near Bos-

Magnolia buds

ton from a cross between *M. stellata* and *M. kobus*, has larger, deeply fragrant flowers, its nine white petals whirled around an exquisite pink-and-cream-striped boss of stamens. In winter, the twigs are covered with the same mouse green, catkinlike buds. A fine specimen of this fast grower, now thirty feet tall and fifteen feet wide, towers above the small white garden. Its ghostly gray limbs sweep to the ground offering blossoms at nose height where the sweet fragrance is easily inhaled.

Bosco and I craved a yellow magnolia, but, knowing that they tend to mature into substantial trees, we felt we didn't have an appropriate place for one. Recently, however, we discovered and brought home from a favorite source, Broken Arrow Nursery in Hamden, Connecticut, a small version, a new hybrid of *M. acuminata* called 'Golden Gift', which is even more compact in its shrubby habit than *M. stellata*. It has the advantage of flowering very late, after threat of frosts, and its branches are covered with six-petaled flowers in daffodil yellow, not gold as their name would suggest. The flowers are profuse, for they are produced on axillary as well as terminal buds, that is, not just on the tips but studded all along the twiggy branches. Bosco missed the twenty-foot native swamp magnolia, *M. virginiana*, that he'd had in his old front yard, so we planted a small specimen of it in a moist spot at the edge of the woodland. It has yet to produce its lemon-scented cream-white flowers, but its foliage is attractive, long simple leaves that show their silvery undersides in a breeze.

One of the rewards of having an older garden is finally seeing patterns emerge on the bark of certain trees that you planted as young, smooth-trunked specimens years before. With age these trees develop bold markings on their trunks, their bark becoming flaked and mottled, and winter is far and away the best time to admire their designs. Our camellia-flowered stewartia, *S. pseudocamellia*, has smooth steel gray bark that is now peeling to reveal a dramatic tricolor mosaic of ghostly gray, creamy tan, and deep brown. The pure white camellia-like chalices that cover the branches in June are replaced in winter by upright dusty brown seed heads that look like spiny cups against the winter sky. If you peer inside one of the cups, you are startled to find it beautifully pleated and colored a vibrant red mahogany.

The kousa dogwood is another ornamental tree, as I have mentioned, that develops mottled exfoliating bark as it ages, the gray trunk becoming astonishingly splotched with pink and beige. The steely bark of our multistemmed *Parrotia persica*, like our kousa dogwood a mere stick when I planted it twenty years ago, is beginning to peel at its base, revealing splatters of warm tan. Eventually, it will form a colorful pattern of green, gray, tan, and white. This is a worthy tree in every season, with delicate branching and chocolate flower buds in winter that display crimson stamens as they open in early spring, best seen against a pale sky. The healthy foliage is similar to that of witch hazels and turns orange and scarlet in the fall.

We have a Carolina silverbell, *Halesia tetraptera*, beneath the sugar maples at the southern edge of our property, given to us nine years ago as a little rooted slip by the California plantsman and designer Ron Lutsko. It is about eight feet tall now, plump and pretty, with charming dangling bells of white in May. In winter the branches of this small tree drip with clusters of dried seed heads, rust-colored, with the appearance of half-deflated balloons. The bark of the silverbell is reminiscent of a snakeskin, rippled greeny brown and cream.

Our native moosewood, *Acer pennsylvanicum*, which thrives in rich, acid woodland around here, is better known for the pronounced creamy white striping of its bright army-green bark than for its large maplelike leaves, which turn golden in autumn. The young trunks of this small, often multistemmed understory tree have the brightest patterning. We have a remarkable cultivar of *A. pennsylvanicum* called 'Erythrocladum', or coral-bark maple. The older branches are yellow with coral and pale blue striping, and the young twigs are bright coral red striped with blue, at their most beautiful in the soft afternoon light of winter.

NATIVE AND ORGANIC

THE EDUCATION
OF A TRAVELER

After I gave a talk to a group of gardeners outside San Antonio several springs ago, a Texan colleague and friend, Sarah Lake, whisked me off to her friends' ranch for what she called an antidote to the fuss and formality of lecturing and lunch with the audience. We pulled on Wellingtons and struck off from the ranch house to lead a herd of cattle from one pasture to the other—not on horseback, but on foot, as was the custom of this rancher, a veterinarian, and his wife. The cows were young and frisky, and I was a little apprehensive at first as we walked in front of them and I caught glimpses over my shoulder of these spirited beasts bucking and cavorting a few feet behind me. But soon my full attention was absorbed by what we were walking through. The ground beneath our booted feet was spangled with scarlet Indian paintbrush, bluebonnets, and tiny irises among the grasses. I found myself dancing about, not to avoid the cows but because I couldn't bear stepping on these exquisite flowers.

One of the privileges of traveling around our country and abroad is seeing plants in their native habitats. I've glimpsed the spires of camassias in vast numbers painting the low fields blue along river valleys in Oregon. I've seen penstemons and salvias glowing apricot and ruby in the desert of Arizona. I've been astonished by native dahlias in Mexico, small white handkerchiefs speckling great bushes, where, also, cosmos in pink and white runs wild through the fields. Every March I thrill all over again to the common European primrose, *Primula vulgaris*, at Bosco's house in northern France, where it carpets the damp, heavy, alkaline ground, flowering in a range of pastels from cream to butter yellow to pink for several weeks. And lowbush blueberries astonish me in autumn when, in mass, they blaze red on the rocky, acid, pine-strewn ground of Maine.

Seeing plants in their native settings helps teach us what sort of conditions they need in order to flourish. One spring when Bosco and I were visiting Hitch in upstate New York, he took us to see a sweep of great white trillium that covered a wooded stream bank as far as we could see. I took in the setting of rich, humusy soil and sloping wooded ground and I thought of our own pathetic patches of *T. grandiflorum*, a few sparse clumps of the single and double sorts that manage somehow to survive in the dry, flat, tree-studded part of our garden we call

Trillium grandiflorum

the woodland. I coddle them as much as possible, adding quantities of compost to their spots, and am excited when one or two flowers appear.

We all know there's a hint of absurdity in our efforts to grow plants that do not relish what we offer in the way of climate, site, or soil. The primroses, which thrive in damp clay and a rainy temperate climate, and the great white trilliums are never going to make a show here, no matter how much compost I lavish on them. But I doggedly cling to the few specimens we have of them anyway. Dahlias crave long, hot, dry summers, which usually we can provide, but this season an abundance of rain and cool weather postponed their extravagant show until autumn. Camassias, I now know, want bottomland, rich and moist, which we don't have at Duck Hill. But our neighbor, Dick Button, grows wide ribbons of them along the sides of a stream that snakes its way from his ice pond through a low field below his farmhouse. Here they thrive, and their flowering is one of those "moments" he thankfully likes to share in his garden.

I am not going to give up growing trilliums. And no matter how humid our summers are, I probably will continue to grow a clump of lavender in the herb garden even though it is a paltry specimen compared to the great bushes I see in the Mediterranean climate of southern Europe and California. But, as I grow older, I am more inclined to grow plants that really do like it here, many of them natives that thrive in our erratic weather and stony soil. *Cornus alternifolia*, the pagoda dogwood, is practically a weed in our woodland, seeding all over the place. How lovely! Wood asters, *A. divaricatus*, are a frothy carpet in these shadowy woods in September. Blue lobelia (*L. siphilitica*), its stalks of snapdragon flowers a rich blue, crop up from low rosettes of glossy leaves throughout the garden near the end of summer. Colonies of our indigenous clethra throw sweet fragrance into the air in August when covered with their bottlebrush spires, summersweet indeed. Wild blue phlox, *P. divaricata*, spreads in drifts and its soft violet pinwheel flowers illuminate the woodland as well as the shadowy back reaches of the main garden in April. The tousled heads of bergamot, *Monarda fistulosa*, weave lavender through the meadow. These plants thrive without coddling from us, and are appreciated for that.

We need not confine ourselves to natives. As long as we choose plants from a similar environment, growing in similar conditions, they are bound to thrive. Many gorgeous Asian trees, as well as shrubs and woodland perennials, for instance, flourish in our East Coast gardens, having come from a similar habitat. Kousa dogwoods, camellia-flowered stewartias, Japanese snowbell trees, ornamental crabs. Epimediums, those elegant-leaved ground covers with bizarrely beautiful dancing flowers of yellow and pink and white, tolerate our dry shade and expand into great mounding carpets along the wooded paths. Chinese lilacs and peonies will outlive us in their stalwart beauty, asking only for some sunshine to bloom. Hellebores, from Europe and China, survive our winters and generously offer up some of the first thrilling flowers of spring.

It all comes down to the right plant in the right place. By observing and learning from nature, and keeping in mind our own conditions, how much rain we have, how much drought, what our soil is like, how cold our winters, how humid our summers, and then relying mostly on plants that grow naturally in similar situations, we can have a healthy, verdant garden without wasting all our energy just struggling to keep our plants alive.

NO TO BARBERRY
AND OTHER CULPRITS

I've developed a loathing for barberry. I hate it because it is planted ad nauseam, especially in its purple form, in gardens all over America and Europe. I hate it even more because it is taking over the understory of our Northeast deciduous woodland. And I despise it in a very personal way because of the pain it dealt me for twenty-seven years.

In my innocence those many years ago, I blithely planted a hedge of barberry (the Japanese *Berberis thunbergii*) around the new herb garden. I didn't know then that it was invasive. What I did know was that it was cheap to buy, attractive at all times of year, not eaten by deer, and was indeed considered a herb. Common barberry (*B. vulgaris*) was brought here by early colonists who valued its berries and roots in tea and medicine. I'll confess it clips beautifully (though needing a haircut once a week all spring and summer to keep it tidy), has bright red fruit (eaten by birds who then drop the seeds in the woodland), and orange-red leaves in fall that linger well into winter. It also has thorns—long, delicate, needlelike thorns. The pleasure I might have derived from weeding and planting those outside beds of herbs was continually shattered by the sharp stabs of pain from thorns that fell unseen to the ground after every clipping.

With Bosco's backing, I finally had the energy and gumption to get rid of the barberry hedge, which was in maturity four feet high and a good three feet wide. On a September day three years ago, we grubbed it out, then turned over the soil with wheelbarrow loads of compost, and left the area rough to settle over winter, giving me plenty of time to decide what I would plant in the barberry's place. I changed my mind weekly, considering and discarding hornbeam (too high), beech (too stout), clethra (leafs out too late), gray-twigged dogwood (suckers), yew (what if the deer fence failed one winter night?), and boxwood (an obvious choice but overused, I thought, at Duck Hill). I finally settled on the dwarf lilac hedge, the tiny-leaved *Syringa meyeri* 'Palibin', not a herb, true, and not native, but intensely, sweetly fragrant and easily clipped into a moderate-size hedge, coloring into a lovely copper in autumn. As far as I know, it's not invasive. Bosco and I still find seeded bits of barberry to yank out in our woods. In the large field beyond our property, we see sprigs of barberry every foot or so. Fortunately, there it is kept in check by a yearly mowing. In woodland where no one is yanking or mowing, barberry is off and running. My heart sinks every November when all but our oaks and beech seedlings have shed their leaves and I look into nearby stands of forest to see nothing but a vast carpet of reddened barberry and the large butter yellow leaves of Norway maple saplings.

Why do nurserymen continue to sell Norway maples? Because they grow fast, I guess, a bigger, quicker bang for your buck. Here again, the purple-leaved form particularly appeals to homeowners. You see lines of them down streets of new developments and solitary specimens like so many burgundy lollipops on front lawn after front lawn of modest, well-cared-for homes. Meanwhile, the Norway maple is gradually taking over our forests in the Northeast, blanketing the understory with its saplings, its leaves so large that they shade and inhibit all growth beneath them. Moreover, this thug of a tree releases a toxic substance into the soil that further suppresses the growth of surrounding plants. To add insult to injury, deer seem to relish our oak saplings and native ferns, but turn up their noses at the Norway maple as well as the thorny barberry.

The ailanthus tree is another of our local nightmares, thrusting its soft, snaking limbs into every stand of sugar maples, oaks, and hickories, and if it is cut down, throwing up five times as many writhing trunks, as if from Hydra's head. Oriental bittersweet blankets the great trees along the sides of our once-picturesque parkways, climbing to great heights with twisting woody stems, covering every limb with a cloak of green, so that our landscapes appear like illustrations from Dr. Seuss. Japanese knotweed, Japanese honeysuckle, *Rosa multiflora, Euonymus alata*, Russian olive, kudzu in the South, all once innocently planted as exotics or for use as hedgerows or to prevent erosion, join the ever-growing list of invasive headaches as our native species battle to survive. Phragmites is taking over our wetlands. Japanese stilt grass is infiltrating our meadows, and like some supernatural horror, seeping into our woodland.

What can we do? Not much, I suspect, for the cat is out of the bag. But at least we can plant our gardens and yards with some thoughtfulness, with some care and a better knowledge of invasive exotics. Every state now has its list of plants that are a threat to the local environment, and we gardeners can at least avoid these plants, even if some nurserymen and landscapers do not do so.

I am angry at the professionals who grow, promote, and plant mundane or invasive plants. Is it out of a lack of imagination or irresponsible laziness? I wish they would stop selling Norway maples and barberry. It would be kind of them not to tempt the innocent gardener with variegated goutweed (*Aegopodium podagraria*), pretty enough in a pot, but an unstoppable invader in garden beds. And, for heaven's sake, can't they come up with a tree more original, more aesthetically interesting, than the Bradford pear? The Bradford pear lines every mall east of the Mississippi, and marches up and down suburban streets and urban sidewalks, admired for a day or two when it is in delicate white flower in spring and perhaps for a week when it turns russet in autumn. Michael Dirr, in a 1983 edition of the *Manual of Woody Landscape Plants*, didn't help matters when he pronounced it one of our finest street trees, but even then worried that it was being overplanted. In fact, the Bradford pear's vast overuse accentuates its deadly dullness in the landscape. The trees look like a small child's drawing, stiff ovals on top of stilts, never losing this stiffness until they are quite mature when, with weak crotches, they tend to split and fall apart, losing limbs and becoming lopsided and ugly. Could our landscapers and professional gardeners not encourage more planting of crab apples or dogwoods or hawthorns or magnolias, all infinitely more graceful and full of character? As gardeners, I think we need to rebel and demand more thoughtful variety among the plants that are readily sold in our local nurseries.

A FRAME OF
NATIVE TREES AND SHRUBS

The time will soon come when gardens around here will be so overrun with conifers that we will accept their lavish presence as part of our indigenous scenery. We will forget that the natural landscape here, bordering the most southern edge of inland New England, is for the most part deciduous. Yes, graceful hemlocks filter through our low woodland, skirting stream banks, and occasional stands of white pine add stature and rich winter greenery to our land. Eastern red cedar, *Juniperus virginiana*, without any help from us, crops up in our fields and dry roadsides, in its narrow conical shape our answer to Italian cypress. But sugar maples, red maples, white and red oaks, beeches, ashes, hickories, and tulip trees far outnumber these few native evergreens, and give our rolling countryside a verdant, leafy, twiggy look, which is very different from the richly dark and dense hillsides of northern New England, for instance, where conifers predominate. Ironically, our native hemlocks and white pines, even the prickly junipers, are particularly ravaged by deer in winter. So homeowners in search of ever more privacy are now planting spruces and firs, conifers more at home in the rocky Maine landscape or in the Northwest, and so far spurned by deer, along their properties' edges.

The landscape architect Patrick Chassé suggests that no matter how contrived a garden is, how full of exotics (and most of ours are very full), if native trees and shrubs are planted around its edges, it will blend into the landscape. This is a par-

Western view

ticularly pertinent approach to design if you live in the country and your property is adjacent to a natural habitat—meadow, woodland, or wetland. The concept falls apart in suburbia, where one's property lines abut neighbors on all sides and heaven knows what they've planted along their borders. Sometimes it's difficult to ascertain, especially in developments that are self-contained entities, what, in fact, the indigenous trees and shrubs are. All vestige of natural landscape has been wiped out, and the new houses are set on bland stretches of lawn invariably dotted with exotic conifer specimens, like chess pieces on a board.

We are lucky to still have wild land around our property. Walking there with our dogs, I've become familiar with the shrubs and trees and flowers that dominate the open fields and the many tangled hedgerows, the perimeters and depths of woodland and low swampy ground. It is a rich deciduous landscape, beautiful in every season, and with Patrick's precept in mind, it has inspired much of our planting around the boundaries at Duck Hill.

We've repeated our native dogwoods, *Cornus florida* and *C. alternifolia*, seen in the wild understory of oak and maple at the edges of nearby fields, as well as the viburnums that abound in the hedgerows, and the summersweet and spicebush we see colonized in the damp woods. Shadblow (*Amelanchier arborea* and *A. canadensis*) is scattered through the woods all around us, and we've planted it here to savor up close the starry white flowers that frost the branches for a fleeting moment in April. Even without the shad's ethereal flowering, this small shrubby tree is worth growing for its delicate vase-shaped habit, its purple midsummer fruit that is relished by birds, and its color in fall, when the small ovate leaves are tinged with red and yellow.

Our native winterberry, *Ilex verticillata*, threads through nearby hedgerows and the edges of damp woods, easy to spot when its branches are studded with red fruit from October through Christmas. By the tumbled stone wall that marks our western border and separates it from the back field, we've planted several varieties, some red-berried, others golden, to cheer us in autumn and provide branches for cutting and food for the birds.

THE COMPOST PILES

I read recently in *Horticulture* magazine what I should be doing with my compost. It seems I am to chop my pile of weeds and leaves all up with a lawnmower or shredder, and add some moisture. Then, on occasion, I'm to fluff it up with a fork.

I—we, that is—do no such thing. I understand if you have a very small plot, this may be good advice, easy enough to do for a compost bin. But with a larger garden, the procedure would be daunting. We merely pile up the mounds of leafy debris from the garden from spring through fall, and let nature rain on it. And yet our lazy, laissez-faire method results in glorious, deep, crumbly, black-brown compost gold, mounds of it, to return to the garden beds. For over thirty years, I have been making compost this way, or rather, it has been making itself.

We use little else other than compost to enrich our garden beds and lawn area, digging it in each time we plant a plant, mulching with it, lacing the grass with it in spring. Now and then we beg some horse manure from neighbors, which we put in a separate pile to age for six months or a year and then give to the heavy feeders like peonies and roses, or make into manure tea; and we hoard our chicken droppings to add to the vegetable garden over the fence. But compost is the mainstay of our fertilizing, and consequently we need lots of it.

Our compost area is near the small white garden, shielded by some bamboo fencing and the low branches of maples and dogwoods. There are three large piles, each partially enclosed with chicken wire tied to metal stakes. Three, it turns out, is the ideal number of piles, for then you have one pile onto which you are actively dumping, one that is resting for a year, and a third that is being sifted and returned to the garden. We accumulate weeds, stalks, and faded flowers from the garden that are not diseased, as well as leaves, mountains of leaves, raked up in the autumn. We do shred some of those dry leaves with the lawn mower to use as mulch in the garden—they make an ideal natural-looking mulch for the flower beds—but the bulk of the fall cleanup goes to the active pile. Pots of earth are overturned into the pile. Small sticks are allowed in the mixture, and the few nonmeat scraps from the kitchen that the chickens don't eat, such as coffee grounds, tea leaves, and potato peelings. We do not compose the piles in careful layers of grass clippings, leaves, earth, and sticks. Nor do we aerate it. The dogs love to dig in the compost—preferable by far to digging in the garden beds—and, in the process, they're aerating it some even if we don't. (Posy, our long-legged lurcher, sometimes will leap on top of the compost pile, circle it in a frenzy, then plunge her elegant white-tipped toes into the crumbling debris, collapsing in its moist coolness, only to reemerge covered with bits of leaves, which she thoughtfully shrugs off after she enters the house.)

I am sure we would have better compost faster if we did what the magazines say to do. But it would take a forklift to "fluff" our great pile, and the thought of running over all the bushel baskets and wheelbarrows of weeds with a lawnmower, or putting them through a shredder, is enough to make me want to go take a nap. For a garden of any size, there are not enough hours in the day, or weeks in the year, for such Herculean shenanigans. I think we writers can make gardening sound so arduous at times that we can discourage people from doing it at all.

By all means, have a compost pile, behind some shrubbery or fencing, somewhere near your garden so that it doesn't have to be trucked too far for dumping and retrieving. If you don't have the energy to turn it, shred it, and water it, then just let it collect, as we do. And if you can spare the room, do consider eventually having three piles. My daughter Kim and her husband, Kirk, who are gardening in Colorado in rock-hard earth when they have a spare moment between work and little children, started their first compost pile a couple of years ago. It is behind a lattice screen in a back corner of their long, narrow quarter-acre property. Although they have only the one pile, and have to sneak the good results from the bottom of it, they are thrilled. The compost is just the ticket for lightening and enriching their soil. It's local, it's homemade—and it's free! I've suggested in a motherly fashion that they leave that first pile to settle and be returned to their garden, and start a second pile next to it this spring. I don't know if they've taken my advice.

On the day last June when our garden was open to the public for the Garden Conservancy, a young woman came up to me and announced that, more than anything else, more than the roses and foxgloves and sweet-smelling pinks, more than the fresh lines of lettuces and trellised tomato plants in the vegetable garden, more than the meadow and the woodland path, what she wanted to see was our compost area. I was amused and delighted. Here was a true dirt gardener, someone interested in the nuts and bolts, the workings of the garden. I hope it met her expectations.

FRAGRANCE

THE EARLIEST
SWEET-SMELLING SHRUBS

For a few weeks this summer, I lost my sense of smell owing to an infection, and I found it distressing. I couldn't appreciate the aroma of the food I was cooking and eating, thereby forfeiting most of its pleasure, and when I buried my nose in a lily or bruised a leaf of rosemary or lemon verbena, when the grass was freshly cut or the soil stirred after a rain, I was rewarded with none of the sweet or pungent odors that are for me one of the garden's essential pleasures.

Fragrance is often a surprise gift, a bonus, something we rarely think of when we're first gardening and buying plants, since we're more concerned with visual satisfaction—color, height, texture, pattern, time of bloom. And yet now, more and more, it is something I seek in a plant, choosing always the flower or leaf that is scented over one that is not.

Sometime in the first or second week in May, the garden here is heady with so many sweet smells, I walk around in a daze. Flowering crabs and apples, lilacs, viburnums, daphnes, blue phlox, dame's rocket, jonquils, and poet's narcissus mingle and compete in their perfumes, followed by early-blooming roses, cottage pinks, and lilies of the valley. It is an embarrassment of riches.

But, in fact, no time of year in the garden is without its transporting scents. Even in the dead of winter, a dried leaf can be crushed to release its pungency, and, with spring's approach, the welcome smell of damp earth mingles thrillingly with the fragrant flowers of witch hazel, viburnum, and daphne. Snowdrops dangle their silken sheaths from green threads and on a soft day release into the air a lovely odor of honey, bringing bees suddenly, miraculously, out of nowhere, humming as they climb up among the flowers' inner petticoats to drink in the year's first nectar.

Like snowdrops, the early-flowering shrubs defy nature in their boldness, withstanding frost, snow, and bitter winds, offering us whiffs of sweetness on days when winter relents and a softness pervades the air. The vernal witch hazel, *Hamamelis vernalis*, as I have mentioned, is the first to flower, unraveling its threads of orange and gold sometime in February and emitting a fruity fragrance. The hybrid witch hazels, many of which are prized for their fragrance, follow in late February and March.

Daphne mezereum, called the February daphne, is a dainty shrub that belies its toughness, flowering on the heels of the witch hazels. It is small and upright to about three feet, with stiff stems of simple narrow leaves clustered in whirls. In early March here, stemless, four-petaled waxy flowers of vivid magenta open up and down the bare branches and throw out an intoxicating perfume into the spring air, a smell of clove, of lilacs and lilies. The tiny clustered flowers linger for several weeks and are joined by miniature trumpet daffodils and early cyclamineus narcissi with nodding noses and flared-back perianths. The daphne's glaucous blue-green leaves unfold as the flowers fade, and, in summer, showy red berries develop along the branches, poisonous to all but birds even though they were historically valued for medicinal tinctures. We grow the charming ivory-flowering, yellow-berried species *D. mezereum alba* in one of the center beds of the herb garden, where it blooms prettily with the earliest of the squills, the deep sky blue, up-facing

Scilla bifolia. All the daphnes are what the plantsman Dan Hinkley rightly calls "miffy creatures," notorious for their inexplicable sudden deaths. They will appear healthy one minute and dead the next. Yet he agrees with me that they are worth growing for their fragrance alone, often at "such an unlikely time of year," for as long as they deign to ornament our gardens. The February daphne is inevitably short-lived, but it throws off seedlings that are easily moved to the "summer-parched sites" this native of high elevations in Turkey prefers. We had a fine bush for a number of years at the foot of the herb garden wall with 'Tête-à-Tête' daffodils clustered beneath it, but recently it gave up the ghost, leaving three babies nearby. One was left in place, one moved to the herb garden proper, and the third potted up for Bosco's library sale.

Always by the end of March, *Viburnum* × *bodnantense* 'Dawn' is in full flower on the woodland path. This upright shrub, maturing to about eight feet in height, boasts no fruit, nor is it particularly distinguished for its foliage or habit, but it is one of the end-of-the-winter treats when rose pink buds slowly open to clusters of pale pink, sweetly fragrant flowers. If your bush is large enough, perhaps you can bear to cut branches in February to bring indoors for a vase, and enjoy the unfurling of the perfumed flowers. Ours, after fifteen years, is finally generous enough in its branching to justify raiding occasionally for a bouquet.

The winter honeysuckle, *Lonicera fragrantissima,* is a shrub often passed over by gardeners seeking bright color and flash at the nurseries. It is a large, arching shrub with a graceful twiggy habit that flowers quietly for most of March, and sometimes into April. The small, creamy tubed blooms, sitting in pairs in the axils of the leaves, would be easily overlooked if it weren't for their fragrance—a delicious smell of lemon candy, which permeates the air for a considerable distance. If nurseries were smart enough to place a container or a balled-and-burlapped specimen of the flowering winter honeysuckle by their doorways, it would be snatched up by the dozens by customers unexpectedly bowled over by its scent.

Abeliophyllum distichum seems an ungainly name for a delicate small shrub that enchants us in early April with its flowering and fragrance. Its common name, according to nursery catalogs, is white forsythia, but this is to some extent an undeserved moniker, for it has none of the stoutness or gaudiness of our most overworked April-flowering shrub. In habit, abeliophyllum does arch and spill like well-grown forsythia, but in a much lighter, more fragile way. The four-petaled flowers are, in shape, a miniature version of forsythia's, but there the resemblance stops. They are tiny, opening white from chocolate, then pink-tinged buds, studding the thin, willowy arching stems. In brilliant sun, abeliophyllum is not nearly as showy as forsythia, but on a gray day, or in front of evergreens, its flowering is pretty indeed. A pink form exists, which I sometimes crave, but I lie down until the longing goes away. (We've almost run out of empty sun-filled places, and, at some point, I have to draw the line between having a *garden* and having simply a crammed collection of plants.) I've discovered that it is best to prune out old wood after this shrub is finished flowering, for the best show appears to be on newly formed wood. Like all the early-blooming shrubs, sprigs cut and brought inside on a late winter's day when the temperature outside is above forty degrees will flower nicely in a vase and scent your room.

LILACS

I am tired of reading articles disparaging the lilac. We are told of its brief period of bloom—a week, two weeks if we're lucky—warned that its leaves become ugly with mildew in the summer, that the shrub has no autumn color, and, what's more, a gangly habit. These articles are referring, of course, to the old-fashioned common lilac, *Syringa vulgaris*, with its shaggy twisted trunks and glorious plumes of purple and white. A native of Europe, it has nevertheless graced the corners of New England and Midwestern farmhouses for more than two centuries, and I, for one, will always have it in my garden. I love its appropriateness, its lavish trusses and unparalleled fragrance. I will suffer along with those less-than-perfect leaves, and the lack of fall color.

I feel privileged to live in a place where lilacs thrive (in our most southern states they will not grow) and have gathered many different cultivars and species to accompany those old stands of common lilac that were here when we came. What the detractors fail to mention is that the world of lilacs is richly varied, and today there are available from nurseries a number of Asian species and their hybrids that offer not only sweet-smelling blooms but a splendid habit and healthy leaves that stay fresh-looking all summer. Some of them color handsomely in autumn. The Chinese lilac, *S.* × *chinensis*, for example, has leaves half the size of *S. vulgaris* and looser flowers on a billowing shrub that has matured in our garden to about ten feet

Lilac 'Miss Kim'

high and eight feet wide. It does not have the range of flower colors that the hybrids of the common lilac have, coming mostly in soft purple and a white tinged with the palest mauve, and the flowers themselves are not quite as showy, being looser and more delicate; but it is more floriferous than the common lilac, and with its exceptionally graceful habit makes a lovely specimen. Planted in quantity, it creates a gorgeous screen.

The littleleaf lilac, *S. microphylla* 'Superba', is a favorite of mine, blooming later than both the common and the Chinese sorts, on a shrub that is wider than it is high, maturing at about six feet high and seven feet wide. We have several bushes covering a bank here between the house and the road. From vivid red-violet buds, the flowers pale to pink starting at their tips, which gives them a two-toned effect. They are intensely fragrant, so much so, I discovered, that a handful of blooms brought inside for a vase will drive you out of the room. The leaves are quite small, about two inches long, and are not marred by mildew. The most surprising feature of this lilac, however, is its habit of reblooming lightly in August. The delicate summer flowers are often visited by butterflies.

The dwarf Korean lilac, *S. meyeri* 'Palibin', is a variety that deserves its popularity. It has dark green leaves not much bigger than a woman's thumbnail, and a densely compact growth to five feet. It flowers profusely, covering itself with small mauve-purple trusses that have a heady fragrance. In October the foliage turns russet and is a picturesque addition to the fall garden. Because of its relatively small size and stellar habit, the dwarf Korean lilac works well in the mixed flower border. We've had it in the main garden, underplanted with mauve-pink *Geranium macrorrhizum* and lavender bearded iris, which bloom at the same time. Nurseries sometimes offer topiary standards of this lilac because it shears into a round shape so beautifully, and these can be used to dramatic effect in garden beds. Our friend and neighbor, the garden designer Melissa Orme, used four of them as features in her formal box-edged garden of roses and perennials, keeping them sharply clipped into great lollipops, and at all times of year they were the distinguishing note. Our new hedge of dwarf Korean lilac around the herb garden is already knitting together and is easily trained into a clean horizontal line.

The lilac called 'Miss Kim' (*S. patula*) is considered by many to be the finest example of the lilac clan. It is a compact bush, growing to about six or seven feet with a pleasing rounded habit and healthy foliage that turns a beautiful coppery bronze in autumn. 'Miss Kim' is the last lilac to bloom in our garden, usually the first week in June (appropriately, when my daughter Kim has her birthday) and opens from purple buds to icy pale blue flowers. One bush that we planted on the terrace just outside the kitchen door fills the air there with its sweetness for at least two weeks.

As for the common lilac—those of us who are willing to grow it are rewarded with an endless choice of hybrids in lush colors ranging from white and cream yellow to pink to wine red to the palest and deepest purples. Our friend Hitch grows 250 varieties of *S. vulgaris* in his garden outside Ithaca, New York. Asked why he is so obviously partial to this lilac, he explains that in his neutral soil and very cold climate it is the only large-flowered shrub that offers the collector any variety. According to Father John Fiala in his monograph on lilacs, there are almost two thousand named hybrids derived from *S. vulgaris*. My favorite for opulence in flower has an impossible Russian name—*S.* 'Krasavitsa Moskvy', or more palatably, 'Beauty of Moscow'. It produces huge flower trusses, pink buds opening to a single-petaled white just tinged with pink, like raspberry juice lightly mixed into heavy cream. Ours is an awkward shrub in the corner where the Boscotel meets the greenhouse, shooting up straight, strong branches topped with blooms just asking to be cut down to size and brought indoors for a bouquet.

It is a myth that lilacs won't bloom if the faded flowers are not clipped. You might want to cut off the dead blooms to tidy the appearance of the plants, but, since they flower on new shoots of old wood, they will bloom the next year whether you do or not. Cutting branches of the flowers for bouquets is the best way to prune the shrubs—and who can resist having large vases full of the luxuriously colored and scented plumes? Like many crab apples, varieties of the common lilac seem to bloom more lavishly every other year. They are sun lovers—don't expect them to bloom well in the shade—and they appreciate a little sweetness in the soil. When we empty our fireplaces of ashes in the spring, we spread them under the lilacs. But, even with no attention at all, they are astonishingly long-lived, often outlasting the houses they were planted by.

UNFUSSY ROSES

An advantage of getting older is that you have the desire and the guts, out of necessity, to pare down, to simplify. Roses are a case in point. The sight of them, the smell of them, can still make me giddy, but I no longer want to grow every bush in cultivation. In fact my rose requirements for inclusion in the garden are now extremely limiting—namely good foliage, a nice habit, no need for pesticides or herbicides, and flowers that smell divine.

Over the years, I've tried them all. I've grown the fussiest hybrid tea with its flashy blooms and graceless form as well as the dumpy but floriferous floribunda and the leggy grandiflora, all of which bloom sporadically through the summer, providing a feast for Japanese beetles. As bushes they are disease-ridden and awkward-looking in the garden border. I still have at least one of the hardy, prolific "landscape roses," the old stalwart white 'Seafoam', which I appreciate for its low, shrubby manner, good glossy foliage, and steady output of white flowers that are pink-tinged in autumn—but I find it without romance, without soul. The landscape rose is good in a sweep (think of a bank or the highway median), but up close, the flower's shape is not thrilling, it doesn't smell much, it has no special allure.

I've grown all the "old roses" for their romance and history, for their unparalleled fragrance, for the rich colors and the

Rosa pomifera

fabulous shapes and swirls of their flowers. But the Japanese beetles love these roses as much as I do, methodically devouring their matte-finish leaves, and black spot is no stranger to them. By August many of them are leafless, twiggy shrubs. I treasure the ones I still have, a few gallicas, damasks, and albas that fill the garden with their fragrance in June and mercifully stop blooming before the beetles arrive, invariably on the first day of July. In August and September, I turn the other way, hoping that the annuals and perennials in the borders will mask to some extent their sad bare branches. I've tried the English roses, David Austin's modern versions of the old sorts, but found them not as hardy nor as fragrant, and, with their hybrid tea infusion, even more susceptible to disease.

No, the roses I concentrate on now have the romantic appeal of the old roses with none of the drawbacks. I grow a wide range of *Rosa rugosa* hybrids and as many sorts of burnets, also called the Scots rose (*R. pimpinellifolia*), as I can obtain. Every variation of *Rosa moyesii* is treasured, as well as the lovely *R. × dupontii* and the apple rose (*R. pomifera*). The early yellow roses, *R. hugonis* and its taller sport, *R. cantabrigiensis*, are favorites, along with the well-known *R. glauca*, admired as much for its foliage as its flowers. For a wild spot, the prairie rose, *R. setigera*, is a good choice. All these roses have healthy foliage that is not appealing to beetles and are handsome additions to the garden picture. They are hardy, disease-free, and have a graceful air and delicious scent.

It is tempting to dismiss rugosas as overplanted when we see the handsome magenta and white species naturalized along vast stretches of our eastern coastline, and used to great effect as highway planting. In some coastal areas, the species is now considered invasive. But, for the garden, this Japanese rose has a wide array of beautiful hybrids to choose from. They all have robust dark green glossy foliage that often turns butter yellow in October, intensely fragrant flowers with the old-rose smell, a good rounded habit, and absolutely no need—in fact, a dislike—for chemicals. The flowers can be ravishing doubles, like the plum-red 'Roseraie de l'Haÿ', the candy pink 'Sarah Van Fleet' and 'Thérèse Bugnet', the pure white 'Blanc Double de Coubert', and the soft apricot 'Agnes', or clear singles, such as the pale pink 'Fru Dagmar Hastrup' and the deep purple-magenta 'Scabrosa', which sport splendid, cherry-tomato-like hips in late summer. Most rugosas bloom heavily at the end of May and beginning of June here at Duck Hill, and then offer an occasional flower into fall.

I read once in a book on roses a dismissal of the beautiful 'Blanc Double de Coubert' because its spent flowers cling to its stems and look then like dirty rags. It is true that the large, satiny white petals fade to biscuit and droop limply, marring the overall effect of the bush while elegant buds are still opening. But I find the task of cutting off these ragged blooms a quiet, contemplative kind of work, all the while surrounded by the intense perfume of others still pristine in form. It is as good as tai chi, the way you twist and bend and stretch to reach every spent flower stem. And, like weeding, the immediate result of your work is visually satisfying. If this rugosa did not sporadically rebloom in late summer, I would just pull off the tired petals with my fingers and let them fall to the ground, as I've seen our friend, the Charleston rosarian Ruth Knopf, do to one-time bloomers. In the cool, damp climate of northern Europe, 'Blanc Double de Coubert' flowers without a break all summer. Bosco's daughter Basette, who lives in Belgium, filled four yew-hedged squares with this white rose for a beautiful and not very demanding garden off her terrace.

Most rugosas mature to a height of five to seven feet, but if you want a smaller comely shrub, cut them back in April when forsythia is in flower, or after their first flush of bloom. Every few years, Bosco tackles lusty growers like 'Sarah Van Fleet' wearing a Barbour jacket and leather gauntlets, cutting out old wood at the ground and shortening the newer canes by half to encourage them to bloom at our eye level rather than over our heads.

The burnet roses are quite different in character, generally low in stature—between two and four feet—with delicate fernlike foliage. The flowers are the earliest to open in our garden, sometime toward the end of May, swirled double or single, not very large, but in masses along their stems, with the heady fragrance of damask roses. 'Double White' and 'Single White' are both desirable versions of this lovely Scottish species. We have a hedge of a pale pink double, 'Mary Queen of Scots', against the faded brick wall of our small greenhouse. Like most of the burnets, it blooms only once, in May, but for two weeks then it is a gorgeous sight. The charming double blush pink hybrid 'Stanwell Perpetual' is an exception, continuing to offer the occasional blooms after the May spectacle, right into November.

'Harrison's Yellow' is a taller hybrid burnet with clear yellow double flowers, growing to five feet. A few years ago, while Bosco and I were walking with friends in the wooded hills of northern Pennsylvania, we came suddenly upon a sunlit clearing carpeted with grasses and blueberry bushes. In the distance, near a great oak tree, we saw a blaze of yellow and, wondering what it could be, we crossed the field to have a look. It was a huge grove of flowering 'Harrison's Yellow', all that remained of an old abandoned farmstead.

The leaves of all the burnets are unfazed by the heat and humidity of our summers. In fall tiny dark maroon hips pepper the bushes, and in winter the foliage takes on a warm rusty hue. This is a rose as lovely in an intimate setting in the garden as it is seen from a distance, used as a small hedge, or banked above a stone wall.

In contrast, the species *R. moyesii* is a tall, narrow arching shrub, eight to ten feet high, more suitable for the back of the mixed border. The flowers are single, with a showy cluster of yellow stamens, studding the long branches in late May. They are intensely colored—dusky, dark blood red in the species, bright scarlet in the clone called 'Geranium', and loud Schiaparelli pink in the hybrid 'Highdownensis'. We have the species in the back of the main garden, where its small, deep ruby flowers are a nice contrast to the pinks of the season. 'Highdownensis' grows in a shrub border by the driveway, mingling with lilacs and the variegated pink weigela, where it is a dazzling sight in flower. Don't be afraid of their height—the canes are graceful, and when in bloom they add quite a splash of color to the garden. In August the distinctive bottle-shaped hips develop, turning scarlet by autumn.

R. glauca is a similarly shaped shrub, narrow and tall, with a vaselike profile. I grow it in the back of a partially shaded border in the main garden, where it is underplanted with fragrant blue spring phlox (*P. divaricata*), double daffodils, and May-flowering yellow daylilies. The flowers of this rose are tiny and very early, single-petaled and rosy pink with a paler center; the foliage is a curious and very beautiful grayish plum-green, and makes an effective background for summer flowers. In good years, bronze hips develop in fall.

The origin of *R. × dupontii* is in question, but it is an elegant rose for the garden, about five feet high and wide, with arching branches of large single white flowers, sweetly scented and tinted with pink as they open in early June. We have two bushes of it, one behind the Boscotel and another growing in a corner of our small white garden, spilling out from a girdle of locust posts. Curiously, in a harsh winter, the one in the garden will die back dramatically, perhaps because this is a frost pocket, while the other, on higher ground, is unscathed. The foliage of *R. × dupontii* stays healthy through the muggy days of summer, and in autumn round golden hips decorate the branches.

The California rosarian Gregg Lowery introduced me to *R. pomifera* one autumn day years ago. He arrived carrying a branch of this rose laden with hips that looked like tiny lady apples, and I was smitten. The fruit weighs down the arching canes of this five-foot shrub, turning in late summer from green to fire-engine red. The foliage of this rose (sometimes called *R. villosa*) is outstanding, rich green with a blue-gray cast caused by a downy covering on the leaves. The flowers are charming, pale pink, single, and fragrant. We now have a bush of the apple rose at the edge of our meadow, where we see it on our way to the vegetable garden and chicken house.

If you have a rustic fence line, by all means grow our native prairie rose, *R. setigera*. It is a wild thing with long whip-like canes and a wide arching habit, and, with a little coaxing, will weep gracefully over the rails. It flowers lavishly here at the end of June, when the other roses have faded, with sprays of large, single rosy pink blooms. Beside it, a thornless version, *R. setigera serena*, with paler downy leaves, leans against the meadow fence. I have seen the prairie rose growing as a large freestanding bush along a dirt driveway in Wisconsin in the appropriate company of bergamot, coneflowers, and prairie dock.

I have discovered to my dismay that roses that are grafted, rather than growing on their own roots, often go into a decline and die after fifteen or twenty years, at least in our immoderate climate. This is the sort of thing you find out when you garden in one place long enough. Now I either buy self-rooted roses or plant grafted ones so deeply (with the bulbous joint at least two inches below the soil line) that they are encouraged to grow on their own roots. I used to have the most gorgeous grafted specimen of the pale yellow Cambridge rose, *R. cantabrigiensis*, in the back of one of the borders in the main garden. Its arching branches of ferny leaves rose to nine feet, and, when it flowered in late May, fragrant pale yellow saucers all along its canes, it was a sensation. But after twenty years, it suddenly began to die, and finally we reluctantly pulled it out. We've recently planted two young replacements, this time on their own roots, and I look forward impatiently to their growing up.

SCENTED FOLIAGE

Several times in the last few days—it is the middle of a particularly wet June—I have walked past the far corner of the paddock fence only to stop dead in my tracks because of an odd fragrance, tangy and sweetly pungent, the unlikely odor this time of year of apple cider slightly fermented. The perfume in the air comes, astonishingly, from the young foliage of an eglantine rose that stands, upright and bristled, to six feet by this fenced corner of the meadow. It is an ancient rose, beloved by poets, the sweetbriar of Shakespeare, with fingernail-sized, dark green, slightly glossy leaves that are particularly aromatic on humid days or just after a rain. The eglantine flowers smell too, but only if you bury your nose in their centers, a lighter scent, spicy rather than fruity, reminding me of a carnation. They are beguiling blooms, coral pink and single-petaled, the size of a quarter with white centers and rich golden stamens. I like to cut sprigs of them to mix in a small pitcher with tansy and apple mint and a few of the more elaborate roses that bloom at the same time, such as the swirled and quartered damask 'Mme Hardy' or the ruffled alba 'Maiden's Blush'. The flowering of the eglantine is brief, like so many of the old species roses, but hips will develop as the summer progresses and redden for an autumn display. And, long after flowering, the leaves continue to release their fruity odor.

Gardeners don't grow perennials and shrubs primarily for the scent of their leaves—except within the confines of a herb garden. This olfactory experience is one of the unexpected pleasures in a garden. Pull a leaf from a bayberry bush as you pass by it, even in winter when the usually rich green ovate leaves are luggage brown and brittle, crush it with your fingers, and put it to your nose, and thoughts of soap and candles come pleasantly to mind. Stroke the notched leaves of sweet fern and your hand smells of the earthy spiciness of hot summer days in New England. Both these East Coast natives are worthwhile to plant for the texture and pattern of their foliage, but I think I delight most in their smell. We have a stout colony of northern bayberry, *Myrica pensylvanica*, about eight feet high by six feet wide, at the entrance to the small nasturtium garden, and it serves as a somber frame for the flashy flowers here. We pass by it every time we walk to the greenhouse or Boscotel, and I rarely resist the urge to pinch a leaf. Fortunately it is big enough to withstand my pilfering—we'll call it pruning.

Sweet fern, *Comptonia peregrina*, is a much smaller shrub, to about three feet in height, with the appearance of a woody fern as its name suggests, a ground-hugger that, unlike most ferns, colonizes in sunbaked, sandy soils. I have planted it all along the south front of the Boscotel on each side of an old granite step originally from a schoolhouse in Maine. It seems to thrive in the very poor rocky soil here, only minimally improved since the construction of the house. Its rickrack foliage contrasts nicely with some dense bushes of boxwood that hug the corners of the house, and the fronds throw an intricate pattern of shadows against the clapboards in the late afternoon. In winter it sheds most of its leaves, but some near the tips of the branches hang on, mustard brown and curling in spirals around the clusters of slender, furry buds that clasp one another there.

Spicebush, *Lindera benzoin*, is a common denizen of our low-lying woods and native to a wide range of woods, swamps, and pond edges this side of the Rockies. It is fragrant in all its parts. If you crunch a leaf or lightly scratch the bark, you will be rewarded with what Bill Cullina (in his invaluable book *Native Trees, Shrubs, and Vines*) describes as "a manly after-shave scent . . . a mixture of cloves, anise, and musk." This is a quietly pleasing, gracefully twiggy shrub, usually as wide as it is high, to about six feet. In early spring, its bare branches are dotted with small, fragrant pom-poms of soft greeny yellow. In autumn, spicy oval fruits, relished by birds, deepen from yellow to scarlet on female bushes just as the leaves become a blaze of butter yellow.

Old English box, *Buxus sempervirens* 'Suffruticosa', is another shrub, in this case evergreen, that, like the eglantine rose, especially throws its scent into the air after a rain. Some people associate its pungent odor with cat pee, and indeed there is a hint of the feline in the smell, though hardly the stench of a saturated litter pan. It is all a matter of association. If you have ever wandered in an old-time Virginia garden on a soft, humid summer day, you remember with deep fondness the rich peppery aroma that envelops you as you brush past clouds of boxwood crowding the paths. A whiff of that smell in your own garden takes you back there. I have sadly almost given up growing old English box at Duck Hill. In our Northeast climate this somewhat tender species is constantly threatened by violent weather as well as by disease. One winter in the nineties, when the temperature here plunged to eighteen below zero, some treasured old bushes of considerable girth in the herb garden and white garden were killed to the ground. Had I covered the roots with a six-inch mulch of white pine needles, as I was advised to do by a boxwood expert after the fact, perhaps they would have survived; for it is the roots, fibrous and shallow, that freeze. In almost any winter, the foliage, if unprotected, will burn from sun and wind. And lately the bushes here are being done in by a disease called boxwood decline. Only a few of our old bushes, nestled by doorways or in sheltered situations, have survived all these vagaries. The hardier American hybrids, like

'Green Mountain' and 'Welleri', that I plant today, alas, have little fragrance at all.

A host of perennials have aromatic leaves, so I will only touch on some favorites. Tidying the flower borders in early April, I inevitably brush against the emerging foliage of bee balm, *Monarda didyma*, and a deliciously refreshing minty smell rises to my nose, a smell I now associate with spring's welcome. If the foliage of bee balm gets disfigured by mildew after it blooms in July, don't hesitate to cut the stalks almost to the ground, and you will be rewarded with wafts of its good fragrance again in the doing, as well as the sight of fresh, healthy new growth in a week or so. Fern-leaf tansy, *Tanacetum vulgare* 'Crispum', which I grow in the flower borders for the contrast of its richly textured crinkled leaves as well as in the herb garden (think tansy cakes), has an aroma I love. It is a smell of deep rich woods brought instantly alive by the crushing of a leaf. Feverfew, *Tanacetum parthenium*, an invaluable filler in the garden beds with its airy clusters of white, tiny double buttons or single daisies, has light-green ferny leaves pleasantly scented of pine. The large, round, deeply scalloped leaves of *Geranium macrorrhizum* feel clammy to the touch and smell oddly fruity when rubbed. This is the cranesbill from which oil of geranium is derived. It is a hardy and desirable perennial, superb for massing as a ground cover, for its leaves are handsomely sculptural, becoming tinged with red in the fall and often lingering into winter. I am particularly fond of the flowers of the white sort, 'Album', which open in early June, enlivened by red calyxes.

Dictamnus albus, known alternatively as gas plant, fraxinella, or burning bush, is not a bush at all but a bushy perennial with stems and leaves that exude an oil strongly redolent of lemons. On a humid, still summer day, these stems and leaves can be ignited with a flamed match for a briefly dramatic show of fire, which explains its common names. Fortunately, the plant is unhurt by this stunt, and really the more appealing act is to stroke those leafy stems to release their surprising fragrance. We grow the burning bush mostly, however, for its handsome spires of flowers, white or mauvy purple, which open with foxgloves and catmint in June. It is a slow-growing perennial, happy to be left undisturbed in a sunny place for many years, eventually developing into a full-bodied clump.

One of the pleasures of a herb garden in summer is pinching different leaves to crush and smell as you walk along the paths. A favorite of mine is camphor-scented southernwood, *Artemisia abrotanum*, prized for its bug-repelling propensities as well as for its feathery texture in the borders. The tiny Corsican mint, *Mentha requienii*, which creeps in the gravel here in shaded places, smells exactly like the liqueur crème de menthe when rubbed with a fingertip. Caraway thyme, *Thymus herba-barona*, romps in the gravel too and, when stepped on or crushed under your nose, has a sweetly pungent fragrance quite different from cooking thyme. Lemon-scented thyme, like lemon verbena, smells deliciously of candy. The low-growing orange mint with felty pale-green leaves, sometimes called eau de cologne mint or *M. citrata*, smells deeply of bergamot and is said by Louise Beebe Wilder (in her wonderful book *The Fragrant Path*) to be one of the ingredients "that endows Chartreuse with its exquisite, indefinable flavor and bouquet." It was given to me twenty-five years ago by the late Helen Whitman, a beloved mentor and renowned herbalist, and it weaves unchecked at the edges of some of our borders. I have seen it in no other garden but hers and mine.

Furry gray apple mint and the delicious-smelling deep-green spearmint are others in this family that I am fond of, as well as our native mountain mint, *Pycnanthemum muticum*, with aromatic bright green leaves that develop lovely silvery bracts before flowering. All the mints have a tendency to romp

and are best planted where they can do no harm in their colonizing. Spearmint conveniently crops up in the gravel outside
our kitchen doors—it is my favorite mint for cooking—and,
although I love the mountain mint's hazy effect in a flower
border, it is aggressive, and so we now mostly grow it in our
meadow. It is an appropriate denizen there for it can spread as
much as it wants and its flowers are vital nectar for butterflies.

The tender herbs that we plant in summer bring a wealth
of rich odors to the garden, from the clovelike spiciness of basil
to the head-clearing pine of rosemary and the licorice of tarra-
gon. We always have a pot or two of lemon verbena in the herb
garden, and I rarely walk by without giving its slender green
leaves a stroke, then sniffing my hand. In the fall, before frost,
we cut the woody branches down hard, and turn the pots on
their sides in the greenhouse, to be resurrected with a drink of
water the next March. The cut branches are brought inside to
dry on a cookie sheet in the oven, not turned on, warmed only
by its pilot light. Then I strip the leaves and store them in a
tin canister for cooking in desserts or for tea. In France, the
tea from lemon verbena is called *verveine* and commonly con-
sumed after dinner. We also stand pots of scented geraniums
around the garden so that we can rub and smell their different-
scented leaves, of nutmeg and strawberry, lemon and pepper-
mint, as well as admire the variety of their shapes and textures.

Surely no aroma is more redolent of hot summer days and
delicious meals than the leaves of tomatoes, first experienced
as you accidently brush them in planting at the end of spring,
and revisited every time you tie up the flowering stalks, pinch
off the unwanted sprigs that shoot up from the crooks of leaf
and stem, and finally tug off the sun-warmed, ripened fruits.
Those fruits are the reason we grow tomato plants, but the
peppery perfume of their leaves is an unexpected reward.

DIVIDENDS
IN THE GARDEN

SHADOW AND LIGHT

We buy plants for obvious reasons—because their color, shape, or texture appeals to us, or because they bloom at a crucial time. But as we become familiar with those plants and combine them to make harmonies, we discover some of their more subtle values—not only in some cases their fragrance, but also how, for instance, their silhouettes add interest, how they sometimes add valuable shadowing or create patterns of light and dark.

Why do we like "black" flowers so much? Not just because they are chic. These moody dark blooms, rarely actually black but the darkest shades of purple, brown, or red, add surprising depth and richness to the garden. Lowly Johnny-jump-ups are encouraged here as a ground cover, in order to spread their deep purple and black faces beneath pale shrubs, like the variegated *Kerria japonica* 'Picta', and brightly colored tulips. I am tempted to add the darkest of tulips, inky 'Queen of Night' or 'Paul Sherer', to our white garden to weave in with the lily-flowering satin white tulip 'Triumphator', having seen recently in a photograph how stunning the contrast of "black" and white tulips can be. Some years I tuck the charming little annual *Nemophila menziesii* 'Pennie Black' into gaps along the front edges of this white and green garden, enjoying the startling jazziness of its white-rimmed deep purple saucers. Similarly, the single brown-black hollyhock enriches a planting of white flowers, or it becomes a striking foil when mixed in with other hollyhocks in hues of apricot and pale pink. The straw-berry bush (*Calycanthus floridus*) that we grew in the nastur-tium garden for many years opened its strappy deep maroon flowers just as the raging-orange oriental poppies were in bloom beneath them, and the darkness of the one flower enhanced the brightness of the other.

When I first wove old shrub roses into the flower beds of the main garden, I remembered the advice of the great En-glish rosarian Graham Stuart Thomas to be sure to include dark plum-colored and crimson sorts, what he called the deep bass notes, to counterbalance the more dominant pinks, whites, and yellows, or these would "sound a little thin." So I added bushes of the swirled, inky, purple-crimson gallica 'Charles de Mills', as well as the dark magenta rugosa 'Roseraie de l'Haÿ', and *Rosa moyesii*, with single flowers the color of dried blood. These deep-hued roses bring richness to the picture and pro-vide a contrast to the paler flowers around them.

Just as dark flowers are effective in the garden, so are dusky leaves. We see it most simply in the vegetable garden, where a row of ruby-leaved lettuces plays satisfyingly against the fresh light greens of oak leaf and butternut. Dark red and chocolate heucheras, now available to us in a dizzying selection of varie-ties, add shadow and richness to the front borders of garden beds where they consort with cranesbills, astilbes, and pennise-tums. Burgundy-hued perilla, the self-seeding Chinese basil, of-ten accidently adds a welcome depth to a planting where it crops up. It bounces around our vegetable garden, and I leave the dark ruffled leaves where they are a counterpoint to the blooms of dahlias or cosmos. Tropical bananas, striped and streaked beet red, and claret-colored amaranths can provide this valuable shad-owing to gaudier flowers such as tall dahlias in reds and oranges or yellow sunflowers in the back of a summer border. Dark fo-liage needs to be repeated in a garden border, echoed down its length, for the most powerful visual effect.

Shadows in a garden can act as vital negative spaces, just as shading does in a pencil drawing or an oil painting. Think of Rembrandt's dark backgrounds, out of which his portraits gleam. Evergreens easily provide that shadowing, highlighting ephemeral plants in front of them. Pale lavender nepeta, spilling out of the four center beds of our herb garden, is illuminated by the great old boxwood bushes, dark and dense, that surround the bench and arbor beyond them. Hedges of dark green are ideal backdrops. The dainty white flowers of *Abeliophyllum distichum*, their subtle beauty often lost when seen on their own on a sunny day, sparkled where planted in front of our hemlock hedge. At Vita Sackville-West and Harold Nicolson's Sissinghurst in Kent, the famous white garden is girdled by boxwood hedges, which set off the succession of ghostly flowers.

On a visit to Villa Gamberaia outside of Florence years ago, I was struck by the beauty of patterns of light and shadow simply created by rows of clipped hedges, repeated, one after another. The Italians are masters at this simple play with light and dark, knowing that something repeated in a line would be half in sun, half in shadow. A line of yews clipped into topiary cones, or a straight line of trees closely planted, achieves the same magical patterning of light and dark. In California, Ron Lutsko plants clipped bushes of lavender in a grid, again resulting in a dynamic pattern of light. At Madoo on Long Island, the artist Robert Dash dotted round box bushes around the ground like chess pieces, then accentuated their darkness by underplanting them with the bright chartreuse of *Lysimachia nummularia* 'Aurea'. The ceramicist Marcia Donahue reversed this idea and used black bowling balls as a ground cover for one long bed of pale flowers in her garden.

One of the most appealing experiences on a garden stroll is to go unexpectedly from a shadowy place to one full of light. Perhaps you are in a woodland and suddenly come out to a meadow, or pass through an opening in a hedge from a shaded garden to a sunny one. The visual surprise startles and delights. On a small Scottish property Bosco and I visited once, a tall pleached hedge of hornbeam enclosed and concealed the flower garden from view. But round windows had been clipped in the hedge, and as we stood in its shadow with the owners, the sunlight and openness of the hidden garden, barely hinted at through those windows, lured us to its entrance.

Steve Martino, the Arizona landscape architect and champion of desert plants, taught me the importance of shadows on masonry. In the hot desert climates where masonry walls invariably enclose a garden, the silhouettes thrown against them by trees and shrubs add yet another dimension. In Steve's gardens, a graceful palo verde tree or a prickly ocotillo might be used in such a way that the sun casts its shadow on the wall behind it, thereby doubling its drama. In the garden designer Nancy Power's tiny hacienda in California, palm fronds and the dripping trumpets of a datura cast their dramatic profiles on the wall of the cottage behind them.

Here in the Northeast, we rarely have masonry walls to play with. But, like it or not, we have snow. It is our spellbinding canvas for shadows and silhouettes in our landscape, tree trunks and branches and wiggling shrubs casting their bold and intricate forms onto the white ground. We notice catkins, drooping or upright, shiny or furry, and the odd capsules that remain from flowers long faded, etched against snowy fields and winter sky. With a backdrop of snow, the silhouettes of seed heads become jewelry in the garden borders, the disk of yarrow or starry explosion of an allium, the indented ball of a scabiosa, the bristly cone of a rudbeckia, the beaded stalk of the sensitive fern. The pleasure we derive from these silhouettes in the white and pale gray of winter is reason enough not to cut down all the perennials in autumn in the name of neatness.

MOVEMENT

Just as the play of shadow and light is often an unexpected bonus in the garden, so is movement, imagined and real. Certain trees, shrubs, and flowers give the illusion of motion in their aspect and habit. The shrubby filbert oddity called Harry Lauder's walking stick (*Corylus avellana* 'Contorta') fairly wriggles with twisted curlicue branches. The Chicago garden designer Craig Bergmann grows it in a pot by his back steps where it is at its curious best in winter and early spring, still leafless and dripping with catkins. The great aloes and agaves of the desert that are gathered together in the garden at the Huntington Library in Pasadena, or at Lotusland in Santa Barbara, appear as a surreal landscape of writhing arms, creatures perhaps from the bottom of the sea, eerily beautiful and untouchable because of their armor. Bent tree trunks in our eastern landscape seem to wave and sway; others, in a line, give the suggestion of a march. Some lighthearted flowers look barely suspended in flight. The brilliant tubular racemes of scarlet crocosmia appear to dance on their wands through a border of ornamental grasses, and the delicate flowers of *Gaura lindheimeri*, perched on their slender stems, give the impression of small white and pink butterflies that have just alighted there.

Ornamental grasses add graceful linear accents to a garden. They also give it movement, not only implied in their loose, fountaining habits, but real, with the aid of the slightest breeze.

On such a day, we have the visual and audible pleasure of their soft rustling as we walk by. In a garden in our town, low grasses, planted on a steep hillside among creeping junipers, appear to cascade and tumble down its slope. In the designer James David's imaginative Austin, Texas, garden, a clump of grasses near a spout of water suggests in its spilling blades its continued flow.

Gravel and stone used in a garden can suggest movement as well. The Japanese are masters at raking gravel into perfect swirls and circles that echo the eddying of water in a natural pool or stream. On a property in Provence, I watched the French garden designer Alain Idoux make a "river of stone" by gathering limestone rocks that were lying about and forming them into a path that snaked down a rough hillside through olive trees and wild box. It was such a simple thing, but by collecting those static rocks and making them flow down that hill, he transformed a wild landscape into an artwork and a garden. The artist Andy Goldsworthy turned stone into motion at Storm King Art Center in the Hudson River Valley, building a stacked stone wall that curves sinuously in and out of trees down a wooded slope, finally plunging into a pond and reappearing on the opposite shore as if it were just climbing out.

If we don't use pesticides, we will be rewarded with another sort of movement in our garden—a bee bending a flower as it squeezes its body down the fragile throat for nectar, perhaps, or the furry brown hummingbird moth hovering around potted lilies as night falls. We will have butterflies in their brilliant stripes and spots, especially if we include some of their favorite flowers—spears of anise hyssop in blue or white, wine pink coneflowers (*Echinacea purpurea*), summer phlox, Joe-Pye weed, bergamot, orange butterfly weed (*Asclepias tuberosa*), and mountain mint. Lilacs provide early spring nectar, as does our native yellow-studded spicebush (*Lindera benzoin*). Even more crucially, the spicebush and blueberries, as well as native perennials such as amsonia, baptisia, coneflowers, ironweed, and varieties of *Asclepias*, offer essential food for the larvae of butterflies. Dill, fennel, and parsley feed the beautiful black swallowtail's caterpillar, so grow enough in the vegetable garden to share with this florescent green-and-black-striped, yellow-spotted, orange-horned creature.

Hummingbirds will frequent our gardens if we grow a few red and orange flowers, particularly tubular ones that their long, needlelike beaks are designed for, such as coral and orange agastaches, crimson salvias, penstemons, pink nicotiana, snapdragons, red lobelia, and bee balm. Don't be too quick to wipe away the spiderwebs that form on shrubs in midsummer. Our great boxwoods are often hung with their intricate lacings, and I know now not to brush them off, for our ruby-throated hummingbirds not only feed on insects caught in the spider's web, but will use this gossamer stuff to line their tiny nests, a notion I find quite wonderful.

Songbirds flock to our gardens if we include berried shrubs and trees to feed them—here in our countryside, viburnums, dogwoods, shadblow, aronias, blueberries, and spicebush. The fruit of native hollies such as winterberries (*Ilex verticillata*), rose hips, and the seeds of sunflowers and echinaceas that we have left standing provide food in autumn and winter. As I passed by our new meadow this winter, I noticed that it was alive with birds pecking at various seed heads, a delightful dividend awarded us for not mowing there until spring.

A DOG BY MY SIDE

I can't imagine gardening, I can't imagine life, without a dog by my side. Gardeners who are strictly cat people, or who aren't partial to animals at all, might consider dogs a menace in a garden, and admittedly, moments occur when they are: digging, chewing, trampling, peeing on precious plants, leaving plops strategically placed for us to step in. We yell, we mutter, we shake our fists. They are rarely remorseful, but always forgiven. Their unflagging, unquestioning companionship, as well as the animation they add to the garden, lying across its paths, rolling on its panels of lawn, sniffing the air, nosing the flowers, far outweighs the trouble they cause.

When I was in my late twenties and first seriously gardening, I had a flower border I was immensely proud of. In June it was resplendent with delphiniums and campanulas. I also had a Saint Bernard, a sweet female unoriginally named Brandy, who was a perfect garden dog, happy to lie quietly for hours nearby as I weeded and fussed over my flowers—until one day she got sprayed in the face by a skunk. Skunk spray stings fiercely, and in her panic she flung herself into the garden bed and desperately, mindlessly, rolled from side to side. I stood watching, helpless, tears streaking my face, as the flower border I had spent hours, weeks, months, perfecting was flattened in minutes. It was my first experience with sudden disaster and destruction in the garden. I would learn that such setbacks are

Dogs in our garden

part of our lot as gardeners, part of the whole cycle of death and renewal in which we are involved. Like it or not, we are faced periodically with violent weather—the aftermaths of a flash hailstorm or trees downed in a hurricane, as well as trampling animals and marauding deer. I dried my tears that June day, bathed Brandy in several gallons of tomato juice, and set about replanting my garden.

Most dogs like to dig as much as we do. Noodle, our miniature dachshund, and Roux, our Norfolk terrier, catching a whiff of mole or vole, set to digging furiously with paws and snout, rumps up, beneath the hostas or around the decaying stump of a tree in our wood, not always avoiding the ferns we planted there, snorting with the pleasure of the hunt, their faces and legs soon caked with bits of dirt. Of course I discourage them, scraping the mounds of earth back with the side of my shoe, but I also console myself thinking we have fewer voles in the garden because of their enthusiastic activity.

Young dogs like to go on brief daily tears—suddenly, out of the blue, ears back, tail tucked between their hind legs, racing full speed around the property as though they were shot from a cannon. Our young lurcher, long and lanky as her Scottish deerhound and greyhound ancestry would suggest, still attempts this once in a while in the small mazelike garden rooms here or on the paths that snake through our woodland. She is not skilled at quick turns, so as she streaks by on her long legs, careening around the edges of beds, we wince in anticipation of possible damage—a flower snapped, a hosta trampled. I suspect as she grows older, like my deerhounds before her, she will lope along in her aristocratic way, following the paths and rarely putting a foot in the garden beds.

If we dog lovers can just get through those puppy years, a canine respect for the garden invariably develops. Through our persistent admonishments and urgings, our dogs learn how much we really care about those flower beds and settle down to keep us company. The bigger the dog, the more important it is to train him. Our little dachshund and our terrier can walk through the perennial beds with the lightness of a cat, and consequently I don't often discourage them. A lab or a deerhound, on the other hand, is going to crunch the nicotiana and snap the phlox. Friends of ours who have a rambunctious labradoodle have looped a piece of invisible fencing around their main flower bed, and the warning beep on his collar successfully keeps him out.

I've noticed a lot of gardeners choose terriers as companions, cherished by us for their bite-sized hardiness and spunk. Mid-sized breeds that are high-strung and need a lot of exercise are not always the best choice for the gardener. Curiously, often

the biggest dogs make the most mellow garden companions—
deerhounds, wolfhounds, English mastiffs, Saint Bernards. These
gentle giants become lethargic when no longer puppies and are
content to spend hours silently by our side.

Until Bosco came into my life, I always deliberately had
female dogs rather than males. There's the problem about peeing. As I'm rather partial to boxwood, lots of boxwood, I didn't
want a dog lifting his leg on my bushes as though they were
gateposts. In fact, Bosco tells a story about the two laurustinus
bushes he planted on either side of his front door in France,
and how one flourished and the other one sulked, until he realized that his dachshund, Attila, marked that particular bush every time he came in or out of the house, and so larger visiting
dogs did too. Low wire fencing solved the problem—Attila
peed on the fencing—but didn't add much to the aesthetics of
the front entrance. But Roux, our macho Norfolk terrier and
my first male dog, is so short he doesn't hit much of anything—
the lower third of a pot, the woody stem of a boxwood—when
he lifts his leg. Friends with male dogs say they can be taught
not to mark their own garden proper. Females, of course, are
not blameless in this activity. They leave bright yellow circles
where they squat on the lawn. If we happen to be standing there
at the moment with company, we rush off like fools to fill a
watering can and run to the spot to dilute the puddle—that is,
if we can remember where it was or marked the spot with a leaf.
In the ideal world, all dogs can be trained to do their business
in rough grass or even on gravel, by consistently walking out
with them to such a spot first thing in the morning, and then
praising them lavishly when they perform.

Does all this sound like trouble? Well, yes, just as children
are trouble, or for that matter, gardens. If one loves gardening
or children or dogs, all the work is worth it. We do not pass up
a plant because it is demanding. Life in the garden would be
simpler without a dog, but infinitely less pleasurable.

CHICKENS

I've never been overfond of peacocks parading around in a garden, dragging their impossibly ornate tail feathers on the ground, then fanning them out like Busby Berkeley dancers on a stage, silent performers until they give voice to their blood-curdling call, which I inevitably mistake for the scream of a baby or the high-pitched howl of a cat being tortured. A few speckled hens, on the other hand, quietly clucking and pecking on a garden path, with a strutting cock nearby, seem to me pastoral perfection.

Why, I wonder, do so many gardeners keep chickens? Maybe it is because we like to cook, and their eggs, deep orange and richly flavored from their diet of weeds and bugs, are without parallel. But I suspect it is more for their decorative value, how they look in the garden. We don't just have Mr. Perdue's plain-Jane leghorns, of course. Selecting the breeds to grace our gardens is half the fun—we've spent hours poring over the catalog from the Murray McMurray Hatchery in Webster City, Iowa, making check marks, just as we would in a seed or plant catalog, for one of this and two of that, deciding among white-crested black Polish, speckled Sussex, buff brahmas, partridge cochins, silver-spangled Hamburgs. For the beautiful blue-green eggs made famous by Martha Stewart, Bosco and I always have a hybrid Araucana or two, and this year we have two French hens (and a rooster), called cuckoo marans, that lay the darkest brown eggs.

Every two or three years we order a new batch of chicks, for older hens tend to slough off in their egg production. You have to order a minimum of twenty-five so that the babes keep each other warm in the box, which is delivered overnight to our local post office, where their peeping raises curious eyebrows until we go down to fetch them. They spend their first weeks in a large box under a heat lamp in our cellar, which starts to smell rather ripe by the time feathers begin replacing their fuzz. As soon as they are fully feathered, in about a month, they are thankfully moved to the chicken house, where we give them their own separate quarters, away from the grown-ups, for a week or two more. You might think that we end up with an awful lot of chickens, but some are given away to like-minded friends, and others meet their ends in the stomach of a visiting fox or a hawk that swoops down in early spring for a fresh meal. Still others die natural deaths. Bosco and I talk about killing an occasional older hen for the kitchen, and one day perhaps we will, for an old fowl makes a good broth. We can't quite face it yet.

The important trick with chickens is not to end up with too many roosters. We have two right now, which seems a palatable number for a couple of dozen hens. More roosters, and there's ganging up, and bloody crowns and raw necks from frequent cock fights. They do crow much of the day, and we are fortunate so far to have indulgent neighbors. Depending on where you live, roosters might not be welcome at all. And despite many people's misapprehension, roosters are *not* necessary in order to have eggs, merely *fertilized* eggs, as the English garden writer Beverley Nichols, in his book *A Thatched Roof*, hilariously recounts discovering when he decided he wanted to keep chickens.

We like always to have a few ducks padding around. Two endearing runner ducks are part of our menagerie right now— taller and more slender than the usual plump Pekins, with a slightly bent-forward posture that makes them appear to be on tiptoes and just about to set off on a run. We had four until this spring, when they managed to squeeze through an undetected gap in their very generous run around the chicken house. One was snatched in full daylight by a red fox that I suspect was pregnant and desperately hungry, the other done in with a shake of the head by Roux, our innocent-looking Norfolk terrier.

For years the chickens and ducks were free to range around our property. They rarely wandered far from what was then the barnyard, returning to the coop to lay their eggs and roost at night, and they did remarkably little damage to the garden. The few vegetables we grew then were confined by chicken wire attached to locust fencing. I loved their picturesque presence, the hens busy bug-hunting, the ducks, softly quacking, parading always in a row. But Noodle, our tiny dachshund, brought an end to this peaceable kingdom. Dachshunds, I've discovered, have minds of their own, and, as beguiling as they are in their comic antics and outsize bravery, they are not easily trained in acceptable domestic behavior. If it is raining, Noodle would rather not go outdoors to do her business; the Oriental rug will do. If she gets a whiff of deer and we don't have her on a leash, she's off across the countryside, nose down, tail up, yipping while she runs, and all the calling in the world won't bring her back until she's ready. The ducks and chickens, some twice her size, were irresistible subjects to chase and catch, and nothing persuaded her they were not fair game to hunt. She quickly taught Roux to be an accomplice. I would find her peering around the corner of the barn, just waiting for some innocent to come padding by. So now our fowl are confined to the long run around the vegetable garden. To make up for their lost acreage of greenery, we offer them the choicest weeds and all the scraps we know they like from the house. Bosco is not beyond microwaving snapped ends of string beans and potato peelings to make them more palatable to his pampered feathered friends, or begging munched corn cobs to bring home after a summer dinner at a friend's house.

A year ago, our friends Wayne Winterrowd and Joe Eck presented us with a young pair of turkeys from their farm at North Hill in Vermont. Not just any turkeys: these were a rare breed called royal palm, with striking plumage of chalk-white feathers etched and scalloped in black. The tom is now the star attraction of our chicken yard, causing it to be *the* destination for anyone visiting the garden or riding by our place on horseback. He thrives on the attention, gobble-obbling loudly, puffing up his layers of feathers like so many upended crinolines, turning his fanned-out tail this way and that, making a thundering, drumming kind of noise from deep within his chest, his pink wattle turning bright red, in startling contrast with his baby blue face. His mate is modest in comparison, quietly elegant in her black and white coat, slender and silent except for a soft

Royal palm turkey

cheeping she makes when we visit with food. The pair refuse to go into the chicken house at night, preferring an alarmingly thin tree branch above it as their roost, seemingly sanguine through rain, snow, and frigid temperatures. The only trouble is that in the early morning the female sometimes glides down from their tree right into the forbidden vegetable garden for a breakfast snack. Bosco valiantly erects ever-higher netting in the hope of discouraging her.

The well-scratched compost and aged droppings from our chicken run, as I've mentioned, are transferred to the vegetable garden beds in autumn. Where some naturally seeps out from underneath the chicken house into the adjacent garden beds, we grow the most astonishingly lavish peonies, lilies, and hollyhocks.

BRINGING THE
GARDEN INDOORS

BOUQUETS

My bouquets are, in essence, a reflection of my garden, a mixture of branches, leaves, flowers, and fruits in a style that is structured and yet loose, relaxed, and a little wild. Making them is one of my favorite occupations. When I put together a bouquet for our house, I think in a similar fashion as I might when plotting a garden. With a basket in hand and scissors or shears in my back pocket, I go outdoors to gather the players for a chosen vase designated for a certain room. Usually I have in mind the primary flowers I want to cut—daffodils, perhaps, or roses, dahlias, or hydrangeas. But what I look for first are leaves. Foliage will be the basis of the arrangement, just as it is the foundation of a flower border, what will give it weight and structure, be a backdrop and foreground, a foil and counterbalance for the flowers I want to add. As to the character of those flowers, I think of some as fillers, offering mass (in the garden, providing a drift of pattern and color), others as the stars, the prima donnas. For a large arrangement in August, for instance, branches of the burgundy-tinged oval leaves of purple smokebush might serve as the base, with yellow or rust-colored heleniums and white summer phlox added for mass, and large dark-eyed annual sunflowers serving as the prima donnas of the bouquet.

I often add a few verticals to an arrangement for contrast, just as I would in a garden bed: the spires and spears that relieve

Library bouquet

the monotony of the more prevalent rounded flower shapes—disks, daisies, saucers, and cups. In that August bouquet, those vertical accents might be goldenrod just starting to open, or the white bottlebrush blooms of clethra. Even in the tiniest posy—of small-flowered roses, say, with leaves of scented geraniums and apple mint—I would add some tiny spikes, perhaps the rosy pink beads of that scrambler, lady's thumb (*Polygonum persicaria*), which crops up along the meadow's fence line. As a final fillip to a vase of flowers, I like to introduce something that arches and spills—a lax perennial, a vine, grass panicles, or dangling fruit, such as racemes of purple-black pokeweed or sprays of green cherry tomatoes. Just as in a garden, the spillers disturb and soften the geometry of the arrangement, give it a touch of welcome wildness.

Even in earliest spring, when all but evergreen shrubs and trees are still bare-branched, I seek out sprigs of new foliage as the base of my first small nosegays. I might use the emerging bronze green leaves of native pachysandra, spotted with the palest green, as a foil for early miniature daffodils flowering along our woodland path. Or the new, deeply scalloped leaves of greater celandine, *Chelidonium majus*, appearing in shady places, to mix with species crocuses or snowdrops and winter aconites. This celandine, brought from Europe by early settlers who valued it medicinally, is an aggressive weed, and we pull it out by the basketful in the woodland, where it crowds our native flowers. But I allow it to grow in wayward places simply because it is one of the first plants to offer fresh, bright green leaves at the end of winter, its rosettes prettily decorating the bare March ground.

Weeds—that is, plants that appear in our yard with no encouragement from us, or that I find in the fields—are often mixed indoors with their more highborn cousins. Dandelions, carpetweed, buttercups, fleabane, clover, pokeweed, garlic mustard, butter-and-eggs, ragged robin, and bladder campion all find a home at one time or another in my bouquets. Spurned in the garden, unexpected in a vase, they add a lightness, an air of playfulness, to a gathering of flowers. The most sophisticated urban florists, when creating a mixed bouquet, now seek out field flowers and vines to mingle with their forced hothouse flowers for just that effect.

Some of the chicest floral arrangements one sees today at urban parties or in magazines and books consist of one flower in one color massed, jammed tightly into containers, often repeated down a table, resulting in a simple, powerful visual effect in the spirit of a modern painting or a modernist garden. My bouquets are usually mixed compositions, but some flowers just cry to be alone in a vase—lilies of the valley, sweet peas, fat hyacinths, nasturtiums, a clutch of violets. Once, when I was invited to a luncheon celebrating the eightieth birthday of a dear gardening friend, knowing that she was beyond wanting more "things," I decided to gather her a posy of violets in every hue I could find of white, blue, purple, and pink. I spent an hour painstakingly picking the little blooms from our wood, slipping my fingers down their long, fragile stems, until I had a fat bunch, surrounded by a collar of their fresh green heart-shaped leaves. It made a pretty present.

Different rooms of our house call for different gatherings of flowers. In our library, which is low-ceilinged and lined with books, I like always to have a dramatically large arrangement on the table behind the sofa, almost touching the ceiling. Here, in a tall ironstone pitcher, I use branches of shrubs or trees as the foundation of the bouquet, and then add flowers and fruit in hues of red or yellow and white, echoing the colors of the fabrics on the furniture and the Oriental rug on the floor. On an October day recently, branches of *Viburnum dilatatum*, its bold dark green leaves decorated with clusters of tiny red fruit, were the backdrop for fat heads of *Hydrangea paniculata* 'Limelight', just turning from white to pale dusty rose. The more upright white and beige panicles of *Hydrangea paniculata* 'Tardiva' contributed a vertical thrust, and gracefully arching stalks of Virginia sweetspire, *Itea virginica* 'Henry's Garnet', its leaves flushed with crimson, relieved any stiffness. A few winterberry branches of brilliant orange-gold fruit (*Ilex verticillata* 'Winter Gold') added a punch of color, and some nodding inflorescences of tufted hair grass (*Deschampsia caespitosa*) lent a note of lightness. By Bosco's favorite chair, I try to always have a small posy. In summer, it might be a silver tea canister holding nasturtiums and single red dahlias, such as 'Bishop's Children', with spires of orange agastaches and the crinkled leaves of fern-leaf tansy; in spring, perhaps, white grape hyacinths and little daffodils with a dandelion or two and sprigs of sweet fern or variegated boxwood in a small china jug.

We always have a squat pitcher or old sugar bowl filled with flowers and foliage on the kitchen table. (Pitchers, by the way, make ideal containers. I collect all sizes just for this purpose, searching secondhand shops, not caring really if the lip is chipped—that can be disguised with foliage—as long as they hold water.) I tend to use bright colors in the kitchen because they are so cheerful, oranges, reds, yellows, and golds with cream and white, and touches of blue, and lots of green leaves. In winter, the small bouquet will be mostly evergreens, the pretty seed heads and leaves of skimmia in its male form, or sprigs of inkberry and variegated boxwood, with a few remaining red-tinged leaves of cranesbills and various red hips from some of our species roses.

When we have company in the dining room, I make a series of small bouquets down the table, either in silver mint julep cups or tiny glass jars. These don't block our guests' view across the table, and the delicate gatherings of flowers are especially nice to see so intimately. Against a dark Indian cloth or the mahogany of the table, I choose flowers that are pale in color with leaves in gray and green. The foliage of herbs is endlessly useful in small vases as a base and filler, the varied rich textures and patterns pleasing all by themselves. Favorite standbys are fern-leaf tansy, scented geraniums, rue, apple mint, wild marjoram, and all the cooking sages—the clustered, narrow, pebbled gray-green leaves of the species and its purple-variegated and golden-variegated varieties. To these I add small flowers of the season, spring bulbs or roses, for example, with Johnny-jump-ups or fragile flowers like those of white *Corydalis ochroleuca*, which crops up in the terrace walls and gravel, and blooms from April to November. Small hips are added if any are to be had, and perhaps a pale weed or two, carpetweed or the dreaded garlic mustard with its starry head of white flowers.

Our living room, on the south side of the house and consequently flooded with sunshine, is full of plump chairs and sofas covered in old-fashioned rose-strewn chintzes. It is a favorite place to sit during the day, to read, talk on the phone, or have tea with a friend, and a vase or two of roses from the garden is the preferred embellishment when they are in flower. Just before we were hit by a hard frost this October, I gathered a few clusters of the ever-blooming shrub rose 'Seafoam', its small white double flowers chilled to blush pink. In a china pitcher, I mixed it with the little white-centered, deep pink blooms of the hybrid musk 'Ballerina', some white single dahlias, tiny, musty red pinwheels of *Zinnia peruviana*, and coral racemes of agastache—these all nestled among whirls of gray dwarf sage, lax stems of catmint, and a sprig or two of winged euonymus, now in its startlingly bright pink dress.

For overnight guests, I like to have a nosegay on a bedside table or a small vase of flowers on the bureau, as notes of welcome. I try always to include something fragrant, even if it's just a leaf to rub, and I play with various color schemes in these bouquets, using whatever strikes my fancy outdoors, often choosing different colors than I use in the library and kitchen— loud pink, magenta, blues, and purples.

I rarely buy flowers from a shop, unless I see sweet peas or hyacinths in winter, preferring even in that dead season to use what I can find outdoors. We do force amaryllis for some gaudy blooms to add to the rooms, and pots of little cyclamens and cape primroses are scattered about in winter. By late January and February, we start pulling pots of bulbs out of the cold frame, and they become our bouquets inside until flowers appear on the ground in March. But the adventure in November and December of seeking out attractive foliage, seed heads, and fruit, and even the occasional flower blooming shyly in a corner, is a challenge I thoroughly enjoy. Evergreens are valued then, even the rhododendrons that I tend to ignore in other seasons. Although curled in their misery outside when the temperatures plunge, they expand their bold rosettes of leaves in the warmth of our rooms and are a handsome backdrop in big arrangements with scarlet winterberries and wands of leucothoe. *Leucothoe fontanesiana* is one of my favorite evergreens for cutting in winter, and, in its grace and rich greenery, an important winter denizen of our little woodland. The arching stalks of leaves, often richly bronzed, last for weeks in a tall vase of water and mix well with other evergreens or the first forced branches of spring. A vase merely of cut bare branches, say of moosewood or speckled alder, can be beautiful in their form and pattern, and often will swell with buds and unfurl new leaves and catkins in the indoor warmth.

I have friends who cannot bear to cut flowers from their gardens. And certainly I hesitate sometimes to cut something that looks quite beautiful where it grows, possibly part of a vignette I would be disturbing. This is a reason, if you have the space, for a cutting bed, perhaps in the vegetable garden, where you can grow plants primarily for the house. But I often find myself buying a plant these days as much for what it might add to a gathering of flowers indoors as for what it will contribute to the garden picture. I yearn this minute for another yellow-fruited bush of *Viburnum dilatatum* 'Michael Dodge', this time planted in the sun, having seen its berried branches recently mixed with pale-pink-tinged hydrangeas in a gorgeous autumn bouquet at a friend's house.

TENDER BULBS IN POTS
FOR LATE SUMMER AND FALL

It is a chilly morning in late October, leaden sky, damp air, tawny leaves lying sodden on the gravel paths. But indoors, sprays of perfumed acidanthera rise from pots and dance in front of the glassed porch windows. And on the kitchen table a small explosion of *Bessera elegans* brightens our breakfast.

Every year we pot up a few varieties of tender bulbs to flower in the latter part of summer and into fall, not only to be placed around the gravel terraces but also to be brought inside. Acidanthera, now correctly called *Gladiolus callianthus*, is an obvious choice. Readily available in summer bulb catalogs and easy to grow, it can be tucked into garden beds after all threat of frost in late May or June, to flower in August and September, when it mingles nicely with summer phlox, low asters, and boltonias. But I am partial to growing it in pots. With no need for staking, the fresh green sheaths of gladiolus foliage rise two feet and produce arching stems of pure white six-petaled stars with dark violet hearts. Two ten-inch pots provide dozens of flowers that, indoors or out, fill the surrounding air with their sweet fragrance. We always have a few pots decorating the kitchen terrace. But after a hard frost has felled all tender plants outdoors, it is a delicious treat to come in the house and be greeted with the scent and elegant freshness of more of these flowers.

Bessera elegans, in comparison, is a tiny gem, a native of Texas and Mexico that first appeared here one autumn, blooming in a little clay pot, as a gift from Hitch. It enchanted me, and now we coax some to flower every autumn. From eight or a dozen bulbs, many slender stems rise straight up about two feet and then explode into umbels of dangling scarlet parasols, like miniature fireworks that might at any minute float, sizzling, to the ground. The tiny six-petaled flowers are fiery red with a central green stripe; inside, they are strikingly dressed in ivory white, striped and edged with red. A red stigma protrudes below each flower's skirt, its filaments tipped, astonishingly, in deep blue. Besseras' leaves are chivelike in appearance and flop about the pot in a haphazard way. No use trying to stake them—they would look even worse. Just let them alone and concentrate on the beguiling flower display. If the small corms are crammed into a five-inch pot in May, and given plenty of sun, they will bloom for several weeks in October. After the flowers fade, allow the bulbs to go dormant in their pots, storing them in a dry spot (on a shelf in the cellar or laid on their sides under a bench in the greenhouse). In May bring them out, give them some fresh soil, and start watering them again.

I have a weakness for fire-engine-red flowers. I enjoy how they jazz up a flower bed, and I particularly like to bring them indoors, either cut for bouquets or in pots, to add a zing of color to our rooms. Two other bulb species beside the bessera that we grow in pots for summer and fall also satisfy my craving. Crocosmia, the South African flower from the iris family widely offered in plant catalogs, brings a brilliance to the late summer garden with its tall, graceful scarlet or red-orange flower spikes. Like acidanthera, it can be planted in the garden beds, and the variety 'Lucifer', which appears to be hardier than most of the cultivars, usually survives the winter here. But crocosmia is also superbly suited for growing in tallish pots. The starry tubular flowers are tiered on spikes that arch above the bright green swordlike leaves. Cultivars are readily available in various vivid shades from clear red to orangey gold. We stand pots of crocosmia in the gravel working area behind the greenhouse until they are about to bloom, which they usually do in late August and September, and then Bosco brings them down to the porch to add some hot color to the greenery of begonias and the soft hues of the cape primroses that summer here. We save the bulbs, as we do with acidanthera, allowing them to go dormant once the leaves are yellowed, storing them in their pots in the cool garage along with the agapanthus. Sometimes, to save room, Bosco shakes out the bulbs in late fall and stores them in vermiculite or peat in Styrofoam containers in the garage, just as we do with dahlias. In late May, they are potted up and brought back to life.

The third flame-red summer bulb we grow in pots is the elegant gloriosa lily, a native of Africa and India. I am astonished when I see this exotic, climbing tropical lily used extravagantly in bouquets, it seems so lavish—Bosco and I are thrilled when merely one or two bulbs flower in pots in mid-to-late summer. In fact, the lily, at least in our country, is best known to florists, for it is grown primarily in greenhouses for the trade. In a pot, the spidery flowers, with their wavy-edged, dramatically reflexed petals, need some support—a bamboo stake or stakes—to which their tendrils can cling. We grow two varieties: *G. superba* 'Rothschildiana', with petals of the liveliest red rimmed in yellow, and the more uncommon *G. lutea*, which is a beautiful golden yellow throughout. Sometimes we bring them indoors to grace a table; at other times they dress the kitchen terrace. I have read that this lily can be grown indoors for winter flowering, probably potted up in September, and brought in before frost hits. It is something to put on our must-try list.

Pineapple lilies, varieties of eucomis, are another favorite South African bulb for summer pots at Duck Hill. From the arching basal leaves, which are sometimes striped or mottled with purple, the fat, conical blooms rise, starry with flowers in green or white, dusky brown or purple, and end in the tuft of greenery that recalls their common name or the topknot of a Polish rooster. I first saw this curious flower years ago, in a small pot charmingly decorating a side table among a collection of bibelots on the screened porch of my friend and fellow gardener Lee Link. Since then, we have accumulated just about every sort offered in catalogs, so that now we run the risk of having too many. When the stalks of flowers begin to open, usually in late July, we stage squat pots of them on the gravel around the old Mexican stone rooster in the yellow garden. Smaller pots are brought into the sunporch and are scattered on tables in the library and kitchen. They flower for at least two months, and their attractive seed heads continue the show until autumn. The pots are then retired to the greenhouse, laid on their sides for the winter. Every two years, Bosco changes the soil in spring before waking the bulbs up with sun and water.

One other bulb that I love having indoors in a pot in late summer simply because of its perfume is the Mexican tuberose, *Polianthes tuberosa*. It is an ancient flower, known to the herbalist Clusius in the sixteenth century, and cultivated in pre-Columbian Mexico. The Aztecs used its oil to flavor their chocolate and called it "bone-flower." A member of the agave family, it is apparently no longer found in the wild. The waxy white tubular flowers open into luminous stars and are held in racemes on spikes that rise from narrow leaves to two or three feet in height. The individual flowers last a week or two before dropping, and the remaining buds farther up the stalk open in turn, resulting in an unusually long bloom period. Tuberoses can look rather stiff in a pot—there is little grace to the flowering stalks. But the smell is captivating, and intensifies with nightfall. According to Louise Beebe Wilder in her book *The Fragrant*

Path, the tuberose went through a period of disfavor in America because of its association with funerals in Victorian times. This is happily no longer the case. Today, it is popular again as a cut flower as well as a garden plant, and its extracts are a key ingredient in the making of perfumes. We grow two sorts, the single species, which I like best for its simplicity, and a double form called 'The Pearl'. Bulbs planted in spring will flower in late summer. But if you put aside some bulbs to plant in the fall, they can be coaxed into bloom in a greenhouse or on a sunny porch for a waft of winter perfume indoors.

SPRING BULBS FORCED
FOR WINTER BLOOM

It is the easiest thing in the world to have paperwhites, the tender tazetta daffodils we associate with Christmas, blooming indoors during the cold winter months in pots and bowls. We order several hundred of the more delicate-smelling sorts, such as 'Inbal' and 'Israel', store them in our cool attic, and gradually plant them, three-quarters deep, in soil in stout pots. But they can also simply be put in a container of pebbles halfway submerged. Place them in a light room or a cool greenhouse, keep them watered, and they will be in flower in a matter of two or three weeks.

This year, as an experiment, we forced another daffodil not hardy for us, the tiny species *Narcissus watieri*, native to the Atlas Mountains of Morocco. It is an exquisite thing with gray-green foliage and up-facing flowers of the purest white, about the size of a nickel. I potted it up in late October and put it in the greenhouse—a cool, sunny porch would probably do as well—where it sat most of the winter growing leaves, finally rewarding us in mid-March with its flowers.

The bulk of the spring bulbs we force for winter, however, are hardy sorts and need a period of chilling before they will bloom. Every October we pot up bulbs and plunge them in shavings in the cold frame. We use our prettiest clay pots, many of them rescued antiques, ones that are deep and range in size from three inches in diameter to ten, knowing we will be bringing them into the house all of February and March, and even into April for our tables and windowsills. It is one of the greatest pleasures of a drearily long winter to have this succession of spring flowers indoors. We choose a variety of bulbs, relying heavily on the little early-spring bloomers in the garden that we can start pulling out of the cold frame in February, saving later-flowering daffodils and small tulips for coaxing into flower in March. And we always try out at least one or two new sorts of bulbs each year.

Just now on the kitchen table—it is the beginning of April— a small pot of fritillaries is in flower, a new experiment this year. We bought half a dozen little bulbs of *Fritillaria davisii* from a mail-order bulb nursery, which I planted in a three-inch pot in late October, buried in the cold frame for the winter, then pulled out and took to the cool greenhouse in mid-March. Six tiny lamp shades, checkered cordovan and light green, now dangle from four-inch stems above broad and slightly curled blue-green leaves. Perhaps only an ardent gardener would thrill as we do to this little pot of brown and green flowers.

Hyacinths and species crocuses are always the first bulbs we pull out of our grab bag of a cold frame. We tend to favor the multiflowering hyacinths, for they are not quite as stiff as the Dutch hybrids and just as sweetly scented. If you bury them in the cold frame by the end of October, you can pull them out for forcing as early as January, as they require a minimum of chilling in order to flower. I like the small species crocuses for forcing, varieties of *C. chrysanthus* in white, yellow, and the softest blue, or the little lavender *C. tommasinianus* and the golden *C. ancyrensis*. They seem more at home in a four- or five-inch pot, more winsome than the fat Dutch hybrids that you can sometimes buy in plastic pots in the grocery store.

Scilla and grape hyacinths are perennial favorites for forcing, especially in their white and palest blue forms, and we always pot up enough to give away some as house gifts. I have a small pot of *S. siberica* 'Alba' by me as I write, delicately whim-sical and relaxed in its flowering, the clusters of fluttery, flaring petals and yellow-tipped stamens gracefully swaying on stalks above wide fresh green upright leaves. Grape hyacinths are more upright, prim, sprightly stalks of bells that seem the essence of spring.

The miniature and early cyclamineus daffodils are charm-ing in pots. We grow yellow 'Midget', the smallest of the min-iature trumpets, and the jaunty 'Little Gem', which is slightly larger but otherwise similar. Tiny 'Snipe', which I first saw at the San Francisco Flower Show, is my favorite cyclamineus sort, with flared-back white perianth segments and a long, narrow cream-colored trumpet. Bosco loves the bigger, flashier 'Jetfire', which has an orange trumpet and a flared-back perianth of bright yellow. It is lightly, sweetly fragrant. We usually include a pot or two of 'Rip van Winkle', *Narcissus pumilus plenus*, which is a tiny curiosity with shaggy, spiked yellow and green blooms. It is sometimes compared to a dandelion, but is infi-nitely more delicate and charming. 'Toto' is a new favorite, often with two or three flowers to a seven-inch stem, slightly nodding, with white flared petals and a narrow cup that fades from pale yellow to white. A dozen or so of these small bulbs will fit nicely into a five-and-a-half-inch pot.

One of my favorite late-flowering daffodils for forcing in March is the triandrus 'Hawera', a difficult name to pronounce, but a lovely dancing thing, four or five nodding pale yellow flowers to each stem with flared-back petals and a tiny cup. In a pot, 'Hawera' grows to a foot or more on willowy stems and has an insouciant air. Another late charmer is 'Minnow', a tazetta with three or more fragrant flowers, the shape of tiny yellow pinwheels, to each stem.

Tulips are the last of the spring bulbs to bring indoors. The early Dutch single and double hybrids, sorts like 'Peach Blossom' and 'Princess Irene', do very well in a good-sized pot; and we always grow one or two of the smaller species for slender pots. This year we have the striped radish tulip, *Tulipa clusiana*, a red and white confection, and the starry scarlet *T. linifolia*.

One new bulb we forced successfully this winter was a hybrid of the lovely trout lily, *Erythronium* 'Kondo'. It was a charming thing, reflexed yellow flowers resembling miniature lilies, rising above attractively mottled green leaves. Not all the bulbs we try are a success. Snowdrops are very slow to flower, puschkinia not as good in pots as scilla or chionodoxa. Even *N.* 'Rip van Winkle' sometimes crumples soon after opening. My advice is to experiment with anything you might want to have in a pot. A few bulbs cost very little money, and the triumphs are without price.

If you don't have a cold frame, you can chill the potted bulbs on steps going down to a cellar from an outdoor hatch, or in an unheated garage. But do consider building a small frame. Ours is three feet deep and divided into three sections, each one being three feet wide. It is simply made out of wood, sitting on a gravel base, with the backs higher than the fronts, and hinged covers that are wood-framed heavy-duty clear plastic. In the old days, cold frames were always made with glass, but the plastic is lighter in weight and easier to deal with. One three-foot-by-three-foot frame would hold an ample amount of bulbs for winter display. The bottom of the frames are sand and gravel, dug down a little deeper than the ground level, and on top of this we put a few inches of wood shavings, then settle our pots in the frames and cover them with shavings by at least six inches. Dry leaves will do as well, or dry peat moss, though it will make you sneeze. The idea is to have a covering that will not freeze. Lower the sashes enough so that rain will not get in, and when the weather turns cold, close them altogether. If you have watered the pots well after planting—and this is essential—this is all the water they will need until you take them out to bring indoors. When I pot up the bulbs, I stick a long wooden label in the pot with the name of the plant so that we can see what we have above the shavings.

I used to throw away the hardy bulbs after they bloomed, assuming they had spent all their energy and would not do well outdoors, but that was before Bosco. Insisting that they not be discarded, and ignoring his doubting-Thomas wife, he diligently started to plant them out in various parts of the garden. While their foliage was still green and their labels intact, the daffodils were dug into humus-rich ground along our wooded paths, the hyacinths settled into the cutting beds up at the vegetable garden, the scilla and grape hyacinths tucked in the flower beds. To my astonishment, they didn't lose a beat, flowering like new the next fall. Because Bosco marks where he plants the different varieties of daffodils from the pots, and adds to them yearly, we now enjoy ever-increasing puddles of yellow and white trumpets in our wood. In this case, we are bringing something of the garden inside and then taking it back outdoors.

BRANCHES FORCED
FOR A PREVIEW OF SPRING

Anyone who visits New York in late winter and goes to the Metropolitan Museum of Art surely thrills, upon entering the Great Hall, to the explosion of forsythia flowering there from tall vases in the niches. This sunlit shout of spring in cold gray February is all the more appealing for coming from a commoner, celebrated and glorified within the walls of this most elegant and sophisticated place. By the end of April, we will be heartily sick of the sight of forsythia, trimmed into puddings in countless front yards, running ragged along the highways, not at all the heralded shrub that Ernest Wilson brought home from China at the beginning of the twentieth century. But in the chill of winter, its flowering branches are a joy.

Forsythia is easy to coax into bloom indoors. Cut branches that have fat buds on them any day in the New Year when the temperature rises above forty degrees. Smash the bottom of the stems, plunge them in warm water in a tall vase or pitcher, and in a week or two you will be rewarded with daffodil-yellow four-petaled flowers no matter what the weather is doing outside.

By early February, our rose-gold pussy willow, *Salix gracistyla*, is showing silken white fur as the catkins' brown outer coating starts to peel away. It is a large, arching shrub that has commandeered quite a lot of ground, about twenty square feet, at one corner of our barn, and I have no qualms cutting long curved branches to bring indoors for bouquets. If you stand them in a vase without any water, the catkins will remain as they were when you picked them. But I like to put the branches in water and watch the progression of bloom from tight white pussies to mouse gray flushed with a lovely coral red core, finally turning chartreuse yellow. The black pussy willow, *S. melanostachys*, has smaller catkins, about an inch in length, bristling and curling along shiny red-brown twigs, and are indeed truly black, not maroon or plum as so many "black" flowers turn out to be. Brought indoors and forced open in late winter, they make a striking bouquet against a pale wall. Our bush, which marks the end of an axis in the small yellow garden, is picturesquely branched, about ten feet high and wide. In water, and outside, the black pussies expand to reveal a deep red center.

The witch hazels are in flower outside by late winter, so hardly need to be forced in order to have fragrant orange and yellow tassels indoors; but their winsome relatives, the winter hazels, genus *Corylopsis*, don't flower until mid-April outdoors and so are well worth jump-starting inside. I love the delicate zigzag branching of the winter hazels at any time of year, but perhaps most of all when the racemes of pale greeny yellow, bell-shaped flowers open to dangle in clusters from the bare twigs. This is soon followed by the slow unfurling from pointed buds of the handsome veined and toothed ovate leaves. By cutting the slender branches in March for a tall vase, you can watch this drama of flower and leaf a month early at close quarters. They are lovely shrubs for the sun-touched edges of the woodland or along its paths.

The branches of the winter hazels are so graceful in themselves that you barely have to "arrange" them in a vase. Just stick them in a container of water and they fall into pleasingly artistic lines. The same can be said for the star magnolia, *M. stellata*, which is another choice for forcing toward the end of winter. The jagged interlacing branches cut and brought inside are already picturesque, tipped with the silver-green fur scales that enclose the buds. But the thrill is to see those furry scales gradually open to reveal satin white buds flushed with pink unfurling into fluttery ribbonlike petals around a cream white cone of stamens. They are sweetly fragrant, with an odor that Helen Van Pelt, in her book *The Fragrant Year*, describes as "watermelon or honeydew blended with Easter lily." (I doubted her description at first, reminded of the imaginative evocations by experts of the bouquet of wines, but, in fact, on smelling the star magnolia with Ms. Pelt's words in mind, I quite agree with her.) Indoors, the flowers, once opened, last no time at all, quickly turning limp and brown—so it is really the privilege of watching them open and of nosing their perfume that makes this preview of their starry April beauty worthwhile.

If you have fruit trees and they are pruned in March, then by all means bring some of those discarded branches indoors for a pitcher. Apples, crabs, and plums will unfold their fresh

Apple in bud

green leaves and open their lovely flowers well before they do outdoors. Flowering Japanese quince is another easy forcer, with a picturesque habit of growth that suits a narrow vase. Cut branches that are studded with buds and they will soon open inside—simple, cupped, roselike flowers in candy pink or white. Any shrub or tree that blooms in the first warm days of spring is a good candidate for dressing our rooms toward the end of winter.

Vita Sackville-West, in one of her columns, writes that winter jasmine (*Jasminum nudiflorum*), dug up and potted in summer and brought indoors to a sunny porch or greenhouse in fall, can be coaxed into flower indoors in the middle of winter. I have always meant to try this. It is a weeping, almost vinelike shrub that roots wherever it touches the ground, and a few of these rooted bits could be easily dug and potted up in October or November. But it can also be cut in winter to force into flower for a slender jug or vase inside. In our climate, out of doors, the winter jasmine often gets blasted by frost just as the flowers are opening in March. At Wave Hill in the Bronx, just one zone warmer than here, it is an annual highlight in the beginning of spring, spilling over a wall, its green stems starred all over with bright yellow six-petaled flowers.

In the dead of winter, I sometimes bring in colored stems of certain shrubs and shrubby trees that, when put into water, will be coaxed into leaf. The slow unfurling of leaves in the warmth of our rooms seems a kind of wonderful magic, though it is merely the magic of spring sped up for our pleasure. *Acer pensylvanicum*, the moosewood native to our woods, is a good choice if you have enough of it. Its striking green-and-white-striped stems are handsome in themselves even before the enhancement of its emerging fresh green maple leaves. Some of the shrub dogwoods are excellent subjects too because of their vibrantly colored branches—the carmine *Cornus alba*, for instance, or the apricot-stemmed *C. sanguinea* 'Midwinter Flame' and 'Cato', or the chartreuse 'Bud's Yellow', all with typically elegant ribbed leaves. Trimmings of these stems will only encourage new growth, which will be colored the most vividly in the new season.

THE MATURE GARDEN

FICKLE

I am a bit bored with perennial gardens. Or at least with the sort of herbaceous borders that we all once drooled over, usually in pictures of English gardens, and tried to emulate, starting in the nineteen-seventies when the White Flower Farm catalog first offered us flowers we had previously only read about. Today, those extravagant borders seem almost hackneyed, overdone, involving too much work for such fleeting effects. Only certain families of perennials seem to spark my interest now, lesser-known varieties of burnets, for example, or milkweeds, or odd species of foxgloves, or old-time fragrant daylilies.

Shrubs interest me much more for the lasting beauty they offer with form, flower, and fruit. I'm excited by the possibilities in green architecture, the patterns and rhythms that can be achieved with hedges and trees. I am stirred by the simple beauty and promise of rows of young vegetables in a working kitchen garden, not the strutting, flamboyant *potagers* lined with colored cabbages and kales that are planted for show rather than the table.

The gardens that intrigue me today often have an element of wildness about them that reflects their surroundings—meadow flowers and grasses, for instance, in an agrarian setting such as ours, played against clipped hedges or a line of trees. Nothing thrills me more than an orchard of apple trees with the grass

Our woodland

high and wild beneath them, dotted with flowers in spring, or an old woodland garden where drifts of naturalized bulbs and wildflowers result in breathtaking unregimented beauty.

My changing interests are part of the natural process of maturing as a gardener, and an accompanying desire for simplification. But at the same time, we gardeners are a fickle lot. We are forever digging new gardens, and those are always our favorites. And we become enthralled with learning and trying out a new field of gardening, aquatic plants perhaps, or alpines, or vegetables. Perennials were my enthusiasm for years, and then, in the eighties, I became obsessed with old shrub roses, read every book I could find on them, wanted to grow them all. Years later, I narrowed my interest to the species roses, the wild sorts that offer beauty of flower and fruit but require little care. Shrubs in general now consume my interest, their infinite variety promising years of learning and experimentation. And

I'm interested now in woodland wildflowers and ferns, a subject I paid scant attention to until we turned our efforts to our wooded patch and I was won over by the delicate and fragile charm of these natives and their Asian cousins.

In my fickle way, the oldest parts of the garden at Duck Hill hold the least interest for me. I love their maturity, how the trees I planted years ago now have stature and character, how the enveloping hedges and boxwood provide an atmosphere of mystery and seclusion. But I am not as interested as I used to be in the flowers these green rooms contain, enjoying them more as an onlooker than a participant. I appreciate their moments of beauty, but I look after them, tend them, with faint enthusiasm. It isn't that I'm tired of gardening, not at all. But I long to be in the *new* garden areas, these are what excite me— the small woodland, the meadow, the newly structured vegetable garden—places still in the process of being created, new ground, with much yet to learn, places that fire my imagination.

Ten years from now, will the woodland and meadow and vegetable garden be old hat, will I have a new enthusiasm, will I be plunged into a new garden project? Lord, I hope not. We already have so much more garden than we can easily manage. It will be time to go back to the old, and refigure it, give it a face-lift, make it new, thereby rekindling my interest.

OUTGROWN, OVERBLOWN

I knew enough to think about the mature size of shrubs and trees when I planted them. "Will they have enough room to develop naturally?" I would ask myself. Sometimes I used a pole, or had a friend stand in the chosen place, arms outstretched, to help me picture what the plant would look like grown-up. But despite my caution, despite what I thought was my wisdom, invariably, the shrubs and trees grew bigger than I imagined.

The beautiful magnolia *M. × loebneri* 'Merrill', a hybrid between *M. stellata* and *M. kobus*, arrived in the mail as a four-foot rooted stick twenty years ago. Knowing it would benefit from a sheltered spot where the fragile flowers were protected from wind and the harshest sun, I planted it to one side of the little white garden below the herb garden wall. In the fall, I underplanted it with the white, up-facing stars of the spring bulb glory of the snow, *Chionodoxa luciliae* 'Alba', to extend the color theme. The magnolia grew quickly into a hearty bush and then a tree, thirty feet tall, handsome in all seasons with its shiny dark green leaves, pale gray bark, and furry winter buds that open in early spring to fragrant satiny white chalices with peach pink cones at their throat. It was a pleasure to pass by on the walk from the white garden to the herb garden, and helped to define this axis—that is, until this last year. Our tree has suddenly stretched its limbs, growing out into the path, mak-

The courtyard

ing it difficult to walk past it at all. I had conveniently forgotten, or never registered, that this magnolia is said to grow as wide as it is tall. Now Bosco and I plot its pruning, debating whether we cut its lower skirt back or limb it up, wishing we had to do neither.

Another debate is going on about the four crab apples in our front courtyard. Chris Galligan, a master fruit-tree pruner, came on the last day of September last year to tackle these trees, which were crowding the path and sprouting long un-gainly shoots from all their branches. Lately, we've been having Chris come to prune in the fall, rather than in the more traditional February or early March. This way the awkward sprouts that shoot up from the branches in summer are cleaned out, and the crabs are thinned and shaped to look their best as they shed their leaves, becoming architectural beauties in their winter bareness. The four crab apples, however, have become much larger than I anticipated, and Chris is finding it more and more difficult to keep them sufficiently cut back within the small space of the courtyard. "I was up at three a.m. thinking about these trees," he said, as he set up his ladder. "Would you consider removing them?" I stood there in horror, speechless, envisioning the void, the characterless space, resulting in the felling of these gorgeous trees, now laden with fruit just turning from dull yellow to blush red.

The crabs, a white-flowered, red-fruited variety known as 'Snowdrift', were planted in 1989 as an entranceway to our most frequently used door. They were small at the time, the trunks not much more than one inch in diameter, and I placed them in generous eight-foot-square beds, two on each side of the gravel path to the door. The path itself, measuring eight feet across, seemed overgenerous at the time. Even an architect friend remarked that I was making it much too wide. But I wanted to be sure there would be enough space between the mature trees for two people to walk comfortably side by side. I edged the four beds with slips of boxwood, bought through the mail, and underplanted them with the early white cyclamineus daffodil 'Jenny', set in a ground cover of white myrtle. For years, this patterned formal entrance has been one of my favorite features of the garden, lovely in spring when the red buds of the crabs open to a spectacular show of single white flowers, pleasant in summer with their play of light and shadow on the graveled ground. The clusters of brilliant fruit that develop in autumn persist until flocks of birds discover them—robins and cedar waxwings in fortunate years, grackles in less happy instances. In winter the beauty of the twiggy branching is most apparent. As the trees and boxwood matured, the daffodils and vinca faded away, unable to compete in that dense shade, but the simplicity of the design remained satisfyingly striking. The courtyard required a minimum of maintenance: a pruning of the trees in September or February by Chris and a light clipping of the now two-foot-high boxwood hedges in early June.

But the trees keep growing, and I knew Chris had a point. I had again miscalculated their mature spread. What seemed like an ample path to the door is now cramped—you have to walk single file in order to avoid crab apple branches brushing your face—and, in the fullness of summer, the walk is dark, claustrophobic, out of scale. "No" was my answer to Chris, emphatically no, I would not consider cutting them down. They are beautiful still, especially in spring and winter. And I don't have the energy to start again. The challenge, Chris countered, was to prune them back sufficiently and still retain any natural grace as trees. "Think of them as sculptures," I said. Twiggy boxes on stilts.

It is almost inevitable that we misjudge the growth of plants and then, over and again, we are faced with what to do when they outgrow their space. When I moved to Duck Hill, the true front door of the house, and the wooden steps leading up to it, were framed on either side by a dumpling of yew. I pulled out most of the plantings immediately around the house—sickly clumps of Japanese andromeda, bleached and burned from too much sun, a robust Norway maple, a youthful blue spruce innocently looking like a toy tree, not the sixty-foot giant it would become. But I rather liked these two plump velvet green bushes. As the years rolled by, the yews grew lustily, spreading to six-foot cubes, rising past the lowest panes of the living room and dining room windows. I loved their outlandish size, their giant scale, and refused any suggestion of cutting them back or removing them. Once a year, in June, their fresh green new growth was sheared back a few inches to a smooth deep green nap. I ignored the fact that the yews were growing a bit higher every year, that we were seeing less and less out our windows. Finally, this past winter, Bosco gently nudged me into admitting that we would be sitting in the dark if we didn't confront them soon. So, in March, we cut them back dramatically, a good foot all around, sacrificing all their greenery in the process, knowing, hoping, that the yew would sprout from old wood. The landing, which had rotted through beneath their speading branches, is now rebuilt, and slowly, the dark, shaggy branches of the bushes are sprouting new green. They are already tickling the bottom of the windows. We think we didn't cut them back hard enough.

We have had problems near other windows. When the small nasturtium garden just above the kitchen terrace wall was new and you could still see empty earth around the freshly burgeoning perennials, I planted several shrubs that I thought would complement the hot color scheme I had in mind. The variegated *Kerria japonica* 'Picta' went in one bed, its brassy gold single flowers at home here with apricot iris and early orange species daylilies. In the long bed against our bedroom wing, I planted the native strawberry bush, *Calycanthus floridus*, knowing that its chocolate-maroon flowers would be an excellent foil for the oranges and flame reds of tulips and poppies around it. I had read about this odd shrub in Louise Beebe Wilder's books, how the shaggy, fruit-scented flowers were favorites to finger in the pockets of the early colonists when they went to church. And my guru on woody plants, Michael Dirr, wrote, in his *Manual on Woody Landscape Plants*, that it was a "worthwhile plant for every garden, especially welcome . . . around an outdoor living area where the sweet strawberry-pineapple scent can permeate the entire area." How could I go wrong? According to

Dirr, it was slow growing, maturing at about six feet by six feet. That would be fine, I thought. What I chose to skim over was that, in fact, Dirr said six to *twelve* feet in height and width.

By the time Bosco moved in, we had a ten-foot shrub that developed huge, almost tropical-looking leaves by summer, throwing our bedroom into cavelike darkness and usurping most of the surrounding space in this twenty-foot border. Something had to be done. Like most men, Bosco is a demon with a pair of loppers. Enamored of the process of pruning, he forgets to stand back and assess what he is doing. He attacked the calycanthus with gusto, and where was I? Not there to confer, to criticize, to screech in protest. By the time he was finished, I decided we might as well ditch the whole thing. It was, after all, the wrong shrub in the wrong place. Fortunately, as we dug up the remains of the strawberry bush, a healthy rooted bit fell away from the main stump, and this we planted at our paddock fence, where it had room to flourish. Six years later, it is full grown (we think), and, although we can't smell its flowers from the terrace, it is a handsome sight from a distance all summer and fall, its bold, shiny, ovate leaves contrasting nicely with the smaller, narrower foliage of forsythia next to it.

At a plant sale this summer, Bosco and I spied one of the new hybrids of calycanthus, aptly named 'Venus', an exquisite pure white flower with a purple base revealed among the leaves in its small pot. We had to have it. For several days afterward, we walked around our congested acreage wondering where we could put yet another bush with the possible ultimate dimensions of twelve feet by twelve feet. Maybe, being a fancy cultivar, it won't get that big, I offered hopefully. Bosco suggested we get rid of the forsythia and plant it there instead, but I refused, wanting this hackneyed shrub still for the branches of forced yellow blooms in winter. In desperation, I proposed giving 'Venus' away to some gardening friend with more land, but

Bosco wouldn't hear of it. We settled finally on a spot behind the herb garden hedge where a ragged old pine tree had once been. We think it has enough space to grow up.

I realize now, almost too late, how important it is to visit old gardens, arboretums, and parks where you see shrubs and trees that are fully mature. Trees especially trick us, for they are often prim and upright for many years, but, like the magnolia, eventually relax into a ground-eating horizontal gracefulness. We have a camellia-flowered stewartia that seems perfectly situated where I planted it near the hemlock hedge, at the corner of two intersecting paths below the house. It is sixteen years old now, pyramidal in shape, glorious in June when its plump round buds slowly open to pristine white flowers that do indeed look like small single camellias. But recently I saw an old specimen of this same tree in a garden established many decades ago and I was stunned to discover how spreading it gets with age. The next owner of Duck Hill might be forced to chop it down or reroute the path.

EDITING

A number of years ago, a friend of mine who was building a house in town asked if she could temporarily heel in here some poppies that she had brought back from her ancestral home in Sweden. I said of course, and we planted them in a sunny corner of what was then my small vegetable garden above the herb garden. They turned out to be the large, crinkled-double deep-orange oriental poppies you sometimes see in very old and often not very tidy gardens, and I enjoyed their gaudy show for a week or two in May, flowering as it happens just beyond the outstretched branches of the purple smokebush, sprouting claret-colored leaves that complemented the poppies. Two years later, I found a note from my friend on my kitchen table saying thank you, she had dug up all her poppies and taken them to her new home.

I rather suspected she had missed a root or two, and, sure enough, the next spring poppies appeared as though they had never been dug. I've had them ever since. These unasked-for flowers weave through daylilies, globe thistles, golden-leaved tansy, and variegated *Caryopteris divaricata* in their corner of what is now the yellow garden, and, although I pull out many of them yearly, thinking they really don't belong here anymore, I cannot dislike their splash of fire among the blues and whites and yellows of this garden. Where they do belong, and where I moved the majority of them (I thought) a decade ago, is the nasturtium garden. Here they mingle handsomely with the May-flowering orange and gold species daylilies. (Oriental poppies go dormant after flowering, leaving gaps, so it is best to scatter them around plants with good foliage. New bristly leaves appear in August, and this is the best time to move them.)

Russell Page says in his book *The Education of a Gardener* not to repeat the same plants everywhere in the garden, and, for variety and surprise, I know I should just have those poppies in the one garden and not in both. But I am not always as disciplined as I might be about limiting volunteers in the garden. I allow a number of favorite plants, which seed about, to stay where they choose to crop up. Foxgloves, the white and mauve biennial sorts, for instance, are cherished wherever they seed, with the exception of the vegetable garden. Here we dig them up and transplant them to the flower borders, inserting them among peonies and roses where early verticals are needed. The yellow

Oriental poppy

perennial foxgloves *Digitalis lutea* and *D. grandiflora* also seed about, but I like to keep them separate from the biennial kinds—confining them to the hemlock garden and the yellow garden. Johnny-jump-ups are welcome in spring and fall wherever they appear, except in the middle of the gravel paths. Their dark faces never seem out of place. They prefer freshly disturbed soil, and so when you dig a new bed, you can be sure these friendly violas will appear. Sweet rocket, *Hesperis matronalis*, has invaded the garden and is to be found in almost all the separate rooms of flowers around the house. I pull out some, but let a number stay, for, even though it is a roadside weed, when it blooms in late May I am happy for its sweet-smelling phloxlike heads of white and mauve. The minute it finishes flowering, I pull most of it up, leaving only a few to reseed, for the leaves begin to yellow and become coarse and unsightly. I allow verbascums to romp, especially the tall stalks of *V. chaixii*, with soft yellow or white flowers marked with a maroon eye. They are most evident in the herb garden, where some years I've allowed them in astonishing numbers in the paths as well as the beds, towering above the sages and artemisias. But they also move about the other garden beds, sometimes appearing right near the front edge, and I only rarely pull them (only the white sorts are tolerated in the white garden), for they are a dramatic presence in the garden.

One year hollyhocks seeded with such abandon in the vegetable garden that we had a veritable forest of them, blooming in shades of pink, plum, yellow, and white, and it was a grand sight. But, as Bosco gently pointed out, we were having difficulty navigating the paths. Forget about using a wheelbarrow. So now I dig up seedlings that I think will be in the way, and move them to the south wall of the barn, where they should flourish, but in fact, stubbornly, don't seem half as happy as they were in the vegetable garden's gravel paths. A few years ago, I brought home seed of old-fashioned larkspurs from Jefferson's Monticello in Virginia. I sowed them in the cutting beds of the vegetable garden, thinking how nice they might be in a bouquet. They came up there and bloomed prettily that first year, graceful stalks of airy delphinium flowers in shades of true blue, then proceeded to throw their seed about in a most generous way. We now have them coming up in the paths as well as the beds, and I only thin them out enough to allow our passage. In their numbers, they create a beautiful haze of blues in June. When they finish blooming in early July, the plants in the paths are pulled and tossed on the compost heap. But I leave a few in the cutting beds to throw off seed for next spring's display.

Colonies of unexpected flowers are the one fortuitous result of my rather relaxed way of gardening—not mulching heavily, not weeding as vigorously as I might, not blindly scraping every seedling out of the gravel paths. But editing them is crucial, for a fine line exists between achieving a delightful picture and allowing a look of chaos, a line over which I sometimes stray. We have a certain amount of blessed help in the garden—Percy, who clips the hedges, and Ferdi or Erick, one of whom comes for an hour or two after work and all day on Saturday. But in the spring, as much as time and my aching knees allow, I like to weed the flower borders and garden paths myself. Among those early spring weeds lurk treasures, seedlings of flowers easily overlooked, or that perhaps only I would recognize. I decide how much of this haphazard seeding I think will add to the garden's beauty rather than just suggesting a mess, when to say no to the flowers spilling out into the gravel paths and weaving among other plants and when to say yes, and then save or yank accordingly. A certain blurring of the pattern of beds and paths offers a suggestion of appealing insouciance and softens the strict linear confines of the garden.

At least once a year, usually at the beginning of June, our garden is open to the public. We unlatch the front picket gate leading into the garden through an arched opening in the high hemlock hedge, put invisible fence collars on our three dogs so they won't be tempted out into the road, and welcome a daylong stream of visitors. We have fluffed and polished the garden as you would a house for a party, tidying the edges, editing the plantings, stirring the soil, raking the gravel, ridding the beds and paths of most, alas never all, of the weeds. The hedges are trimmed into those strict geometric lines that contain the exuberant flowering. For a brief moment, we sigh with satisfaction, pat ourselves a bit on the back, and enjoy our visitors' appreciation.

It is seldom like this. In early spring, the garden is raw, riddled with chickweed and celandine, its straight lines dented and shaggy, its hedges unclipped, the gravel paths thick with seedlings. Thankfully, after winter's hibernation, we are fired up with energy, wanting to be outside working more than anything else (it is in spring, muscles aching, knees caked with dirt, that I am my happiest self), thrilling to each new appearance of leaf and flower. With our youthful helpers, we gradually transform the garden, make right those edges and hedges, and conquer that first onslaught of weeds.

Sometime in July, when the garden is still tidy and in its early summer prime, with lettuces and root crops burgeoning in the vegetable garden, daylilies and scented Asiatic lilies opening their starry trumpets, we turn our backs and leave. For two weeks, we go to Bosco's house in France, abandoning our creation here for a smaller garden there. Each year, feeling wrenched, I wonder if I can bear to go, bear to miss the daily occurrences, the fleeting flowerings. No one, not even gardening friends to whom I mutter, seems in the least sympathetic, knowing I'm headed for a vacation in that slow-paced, agricultural, beauty-loving, food-obsessed French world.

We leave the garden in tip-top shape and come home to a virtual jungle. Yes, the lawns are mowed while we are gone, the hedges clipped, and the most obvious weeds pulled by our faithful part-time helpers. But, in the mere two weeks we're away, the random seeding that seemed so charming in May and June is out of control, a mess of sprawling plants and spent spring bloomers. Appalled, overcome with the work involved in getting the garden back in order, knowing that in fact I will not completely get it back in order this season, I wonder, yearly, if the garden I've made and love above all others is more than we can handle. Once we've begun to tackle the mess, bit by bit, the satisfying evidence of our slow progress calms me.

Ruthless editing is the key. Taking one section of the garden at a time, I stand back to assess the overgrowth, deciding where the profusion is still effective, where just chaotic. I pull out clumps of *Scabiosa ochroleuca* that are trying to take over the kitchen terrace, along with several bushel baskets of spearmint. Black-eyed Susans in the middle of paths are yanked. Johnny-jump-ups, spry and fetching all spring, are now leggy, their lower leaves tattered and brown, their tops only flowering shyly as they climb and weave into other plants. Out they go. Feverfew has gone to seed and needs to be cut back or pulled. Nepeta and lady's mantle could use a shearing almost to the ground. Perilla (where did it come from?) needs to be pulled, unless its dark plum foliage is contributing a needed depth to a color harmony. Flopping perennials need subtle propping and staking with twigs and branches. If we don't have a heat wave that drives me inside, gradually, inch by inch, the work gets done and a certain suggestion of order is restored.

By September and October, a new freshness veils the garden, as the humid dog days of summer are replaced by sparkling blue sky and gentle sun. The plants that flowered in June offer new blooms and leaves deepen into warm, vibrant hues. The wilder, overgrown look of the flower borders and shrubbery seems a natural accompaniment to the season. But by early November, I sigh with relief as spent perennials get cut down and carted off, leaving only the golden grasses and amsonias, and I can savor the bones of the gardens, the now twiggy shrubs still showing a hint of brilliant leaf, roses revealing their reddened canes and rosy hips, the hedges and boxwood giving the garden its form and substance.

On an early November day recently, returning with the dogs from a walk in the fields just before dusk, the afternoon light low-slung and golden, I approached the house through our spit of woods, and savored its simpler, bare-branched beauty and the lingering patches of rich green on the ground: ferns—the lady ferns and holly ferns that are slow to die back, and the evergreen Christmas ferns; puddles of glossy-leaved epimediums, some rich green, others russet; fresh green, pebbly-leaved bouquets of foxgloves; and the dark-fingered leaves of hellebores. I made a mental note to lift and divide some of the epimediums to spread along the secondary paths and plant many more ferns.

AN APOLOGY
TO CHRISTOPHER LLOYD

You were right after all, Christopher Lloyd. Over time, a herb garden *can* easily dissolve into a "sentimental mess." If you were standing in ours at midsummer, you'd say, See, what did I tell you?

Writing in my book *Duck Hill Journal*, with passion and innocence, I chastised the great gardener and garden writer for dismissing herb gardens as such. I didn't admit that the herb enthusiast can get so carried away with the lore of these plants that little regard is given to whether they are worthy garden dwellers or not. But in my travels I had seen many gardens of herbs in their prime that impressed me with their beauty of pattern and marriages of gray and green. And when I wrote those words of protest more than twenty years ago, the herb garden at Duck Hill was fresh and prim, its sensual denizens young and shapely, its pattern of beds still cleanly delineated. Now, with age, this garden takes on an air of unruliness, especially in the dog days of summer.

Although some herbs are generally tidy in habit and have a structural presence—santolina, for example, germander, lavender, rue, and southernwood—many more tend to either sprawl or run rampant. We have two kinds of comfrey in the garden, given to me by colleagues who, I suspect, had plenty to share. One, a cultivar called 'Hidcote Blue', is bold-leaved with gorgeous sky blue nodding bells, flowering for many weeks in May and June. How can I not like it? The other is unnamed, a low-growing, ground-eating sort with pretty white flowers touched with rose pink. Valued medicinally for centuries, the comfreys are worthy garden plants, with foliage that stays healthy all summer. But they are "vigorous," as the books delicately put it, and have spread far beyond what I intended.

Apple mint runs through the back of one border, and as much as I like its furry pale gray rounded leaves, I have to yank out yards of it, its white roots snaking through all its neighbors. Garlic chives, *Allium tuberosum*, look like onion grass in spring, and seed about the garden pervasively. The little bulbs are devilish to weed out of the gravel paths and beds, where they crop up in mats of thyme and pinks. When they bloom with starry white heads in September, almost all is forgiven. Fern-leaf tansy, one of my favorites in the garden and for bouquets because of its crinkly-textured dark green leaves smelling of pine and the woods, is almost as much a thug as apple mint. By late summer, all the lower leaves on its three-foot stalks have shriveled and turned brown, and the only solution is to cut it down to the ground, forfeiting any heads of still-green leaves. The creeping thymes have obliterated the edges to this patterned garden. So have the charming cottage pinks, as well as wild oregano and lady's mantle, which prefers the gravel of the paths to the beds. Dusty pink lily of the valley has escaped the shadowy back reaches of the garden and woven its way out to the path and sunlight.

Then there's Betsy Sluder's grandmother's thornless rose. Does that sound sentimental enough? A rooted sprig of this smooth-caned mystery rose was given to me years ago by the above-mentioned Betsy, who was a renowned gardener in Armonk, New York. Her rose has taken over a section of the garden about eight feet wide by six feet deep, cohabiting with bee balm and sweet cicely. When it blooms in June with intensely fragrant, small, cabbagelike blush pink flowers, I am enchanted. In July the red-flowering monarda and the ferny sweet cicely compensate for its dullness. By August, this area of the garden has nothing to recommend it, the monarda mildewed, the sweet cicely yellowing at the edges. The apothecary rose, *Rosa gallica officinalis*, is on its own roots and runs in a similar way in another back bed of the herb garden. And again, when it is covered in perfumed lipstick-pink saucers with golden stamens, I am thrilled to have it in such abundance. But by midsummer these romantic rose blooms are mere memories, and I am faced with a thicket of ratty, spotted leaves.

The solution is to dig up the whole mess, turn over and enrich the soil, pull apart the lusty perennials, replant only the healthiest pieces, discard half of the rose rootings—in short, to start all over again. I am exhausted at the thought of it.

The great old box bushes that mark this garden's paths are its salvation, along with the strict frame of the clipped hedge. They give it a steadiness, a semblance of order. And, in April, when scillas create pools of blue, and early yellow tulips rise above the soft, feathery green of southernwood; in May and June, when dianthus fills the air with spice, and spires of foxgloves, dittany, and mulleins contrast with spheres of alliums and swirled rose blooms; in summer, when the thymes throw their pungent scent into the turgid air and hummingbirds whiz about the shaggy heads of the bee balm, when fat clumps of scented geraniums offer every imaginable pattern of leaf and scent, and the purple and golden sages create ribbons of color, I would say to Christopher Lloyd, it is a sentimental mess that gives much pleasure.

UNDER THE WEATHER

It is late September, and I have been laid low all week with the flu while rain came down in buckets outside, the aftermath of a hurricane worrying the southern coast. Yesterday, finally, with sun straining through heavy clouds, I shambled outdoors for a walk through the garden. Instead of being cheered, instead of savoring its incidental beauty, I became increasingly depressed by its air of disarray as I went along. The rain had beaten down anything that would still be standing now, and everywhere I went, I had to duck, squeeze by, step over. I looked around at the garden as one does after being away for a while, and had for a moment an outsider's view, unbiased, objective. Sometimes, at moments like this, I am astonished by its good bones and beauty, but yesterday I thought how cluttered the garden was, like a table with too many bibelots on it, busy, bitsy, fussy, crammed. Where was the serenity? Perennials flip-flopping all over the place. Trees and shrubs jostling, overshadowing, nudging, leaning into paths, not one of them given enough room really, not to spread its wings. How could I have done this, I asked myself, I who was supposed to know, to understand a thing or two, about garden design? Why had I acquired, willingly, so many plants? Where were the needed blank spaces, the simple planes?

I came inside discouraged, exhausted, downhearted. Let it snow, I mumbled to myself as I climbed back into bed. Let it all go away, this verdant overgrowth. Bring on the spareness of winter, and then the cleanness, the uprightness of spring.

Part of my reaction to the garden yesterday was due to feeling unwell. But not all. The garden *is* cluttered, more than I would like, and I will have to think hard about simplifying it. And it has, just now, a look of abandonment. I knew that the unruliness that depressed me was not due wholly to a summer of rain or the dishevelment of autumn. Inevitably, as the days and evenings turn cold, when autumn is in the air, my thoughts turn inward. I begin to think more about fluffing my nest, cleaning out closets and drawers (spring cleaning, after all, is focused solely out of doors), cooking hearty meals, reading books, slipcovering tattered furniture. In so doing, I turn my back on the garden, desert it when it needs my attention. But then, seeing it ragged at the edges, as it appears when we return home in July and again now, is deeply unsettling. For, to a large extent, my happiness depends on that interaction with the garden, that act of forming, tending, of intimately observing and being involved in its ever-changing process, the birth, maturing, aging, death, and rebirth that is its constant theme.

This morning the sky is deep blue, the sun strong, the air crisp, and I spent about an hour tying up wayward canes of climbing and species roses along our paddock fence. It felt good to feel the sun on my face once more, and even my small amount of work made for a more orderly appearance of these naturally wild-looking shrubs and gave me satisfaction. As I walked back down to the house through the yellow garden, I stopped to watch a goldfinch swaying on the small heads of perennial sunflowers, his buttercup yellow summer coat now streaked with the pea green that will be his full winter dress. I continued to the herb garden and found myself admiring its neatly hedged-in profuseness, admiring the great balls of boxwood that give it weight, their shadowed sides darkly, richly green, their rounded heads lit by the sun and glistening. Set against their dark mass, pink and white bells of *Nicotiana mutabilis* danced and spires of late summer salvias and chaste trees frothed with blue. The garden sparkled with light and shadow, with life, and I did not notice the encroaching, invading flanks of shrubbery, the louche perennials.

If I were giving advice to a young gardener, one who, like us, is crazy about plants, I would say, Remember the structure of the garden, and be sure to include the shrubs and trees that hold it together. If it is a woodland garden, add shade-loving shrubs for year-round interest, a few of them evergreen to brighten the brownness in winter. Include understory trees, the shads and dogwoods and redbuds that give it grace. If it is a garden of flower beds, consider its pattern, its tracery of paths, and perhaps add hedges to contain and compartmentalize it, and, as in ours, balls of evergreens for punctuation. Then, even in times of neglect, even when it's under the weather, these good bones will redeem your garden.

PRESCRIPTIONS FOR THE AGING GARDENER

SHRUBS VERSUS PERENNIALS

We don't realize in the beginning how much work most perennials are. A few, like peonies, hostas, and *Dictamnus albus*, survive with a minimum of care, expanding obligingly in volume and flowering with abandon as long as they are in a situation they like (sun and rich soil for peonies and the gas plant; moist, humusy shade for hostas). But most herbaceous perennials benefit from frequent division and replanting in enriched soil, ideally every three years or so, in order to maintain healthy foliage and robust flowers. Many want careful deadheading after they flower to encourage a flush of secondary blooms, and some, like lady's mantle, bee balm, and even daylilies, can get so ratty-looking in high summer, it is best to cut them down almost to the ground to encourage fresh new leaf growth.

A number of perennials require some means of support, thanks to our violent summer storms. I resist this task as long as I can, for I like a certain amount of leaning and flopping, but when our precious blooms are facedown in the dirt, there's no recourse but to give them an artificial lift. Staking is an art in itself—coaxing the stalks and stems into a gentle attitude of uprightness, propping with twigs and twine while still allowing a certain amount of their natural tendency to arch or lean. I wince to see flower borders where perennials are braced like soldiers, ramrod straight, regimented into blocks with wire, tied at the neck and waist with string, without a trace left of their natural grace or charm.

Some perennials are not very perennial at all but in fact disappear after a couple of years if they haven't seeded around before expiring. Suddenly, I wonder where the columbines went, and whatever happened to the blue flax and the pasqueflowers. Others, among them the adored thugs I've mentioned, notoriously run by stolons or ever-expanding roots, overcoming more sedate neighbors, which then quietly give up the ghost. I love the perennials that seed about, but they often crop up where you don't particularly want them and then need to be moved. This is all work, endless work.

Shrubs, on the other hand, behave themselves, demanding a minimum of effort once they're planted. For one thing, they stay put. A few, like clethra, will colonize into a generous clump, and almost all develop stouter girths than we anticipate. But they don't show up where you didn't plant them. They don't die out, not unless they were unsuitably placed from the start, in the wrong climate or soil, or in sun when they should be in shade, or in shade when they should be in sun. They don't need staking. They never have to be divided. And they don't require deadheading; in fact, their flowers often devolve into picturesque seed heads and are followed by ornamental fruit that would be lost in doing so.

This past fall, I visited the exceptional garden of Courtney Daniels in Virginia. She had created a series of hedged-in garden rooms around her house, each with a particular color scheme, similar to ours at Duck Hill. But there was barely a perennial in sight. The borders within those rooms were filled with shrubs and grasses. Viburnums, dogwoods, hydrangeas, abelias, pennisetums, molinias, panicums. With artistry she combined the fruits and flowers of shrubs with contrasting leaf textures and unusual leaf color, adding chartreuse foliage and creamy variegation in her yellow garden, burgundy-and-plum-splashed leaves in her red garden. Dwarf evergreens and boxwood were woven in among the woody shrubs for contrast. Sweeps and clumps of ornamental grasses provided a graceful linear pattern. (I suspect spring bulbs had been scattered beneath the shrubs.) My friend had mulched the beds with shredded bark to hold in the moisture in summer and discourage weeds. But you didn't notice it much beneath the lacing of branches. Eventually some of the shrubs, I knew, would outgrow their spots and have to be removed or replaced. But this was a garden, I realized, offering beauty and interest through every season with considerably less maintenance than mine demanded.

Perhaps we're not willing to give up all our perennials. But as we age, slowly replacing some of the more demanding sorts in our borders with small shrubs is a prudent measure. Bosco and I are beginning to transform the main garden with generous additions of woody plants—abelia, shrub dogwoods, more rugosa roses, hydrangeas. Last spring we removed some stands of summer phlox (mildewed foliage, needs constant dividing, requires attentive deadheading to ensure rebloom and prevent seedlings that revert to their more natural mingy blue-pink), despite loving their lavish flower heads and peppery fragrance. In their place, we planted late summer hydrangeas, charming paniculata sorts like the compact 'Little Lamb', white aging to soft pink, and early-flowering 'Dharuma'. The hydrangeas will demand nothing but admiration.

HIGH GRASS VERSUS LAWN

I wouldn't want to be without any lawn. Nothing sets off a garden of flowers more beautifully than that calm, unbusied, velvet expanse. Furthermore, I love to rest on it, propped up on my elbows, and watch my dogs sprawl beside me, their back legs stretched out so their bellies are flattened against the soft coolness of the grass. But a lawn requires constant maintenance, even a less-than-perfect one like ours, threaded through with clover, ground ivy, and slender speedwell. Once-a-week mowing is necessary to preserve that velvet nap, unless we are having a drought, when the lawn turns brown and crisp anyway without constant watering. As much as we love the smell of a newly mowed lawn, and the elegant look of its parallel lines of fresh-cut green, the whining, whirring racket of weekly noise from the mower disrupts the peace of our Eden, spewing fumes that are much more of a detriment to our atmosphere than most of us realize. According to a study by the California Environmental Protection Agency, a gasoline-powered lawnmower running for an hour pollutes our air about as much as forty new cars would, driven for the same amount of time. And I shudder to think of the vast amounts of pesticides and herbicides indiscriminately showered on suburban yards by lawn companies, often innocently enough contracted by homeowners who merely want a dandelion-free expanse of green or think ticks lurk there (the ticks that carry Lyme disease are more apt to be in our woods and rough fields) and haven't considered the consequences.

At a dinner party recently, our hostess asked each guest to offer an idea of how we might personally help combat global warming. There was talk of lightbulbs and hybrid cars and recycling. When my turn came, thinking I should say something gardenesque, I suggested giving a piece of our yards over to high grass, or a flowering meadow, no matter how small.

We have a friend who has a small suburban garden, at most a quarter of an acre, and below her house and terrace, bordered by espaliered apples, lilies, and herbs, she has a tiny meadow, merely grass allowed to grow tall and splattered with wildflowers. It is surprising to see this bit of wildness in such a confined and structured space, and its effect is charming.

Even grass that is kept only slightly higher played against closely mowed turf can create alluring patterns and contrasts of texture. I remember a small hedged-in garden in Scotland where the grass was perhaps six or eight inches high, and nar-

The mini-meadow

row paths were closely mowed through it like runners of carpet, straight down the center of the garden and then off in diagonals. Stone pots of flowers stood in the higher grass where the central path and the diagonal paths met. The garden was delightful in its simplicity, the different heights of grass creating an imaginative pattern of lines and textures, and the pots, like punctuation marks, drawing your eye down the garden's central path to an arched gap in the hedge at the far end.

Bosco and I visited another garden this summer, in Normandy, where blocks of meadow were divided by broad, crisscrossing paths of lawn in which apple trees stood. The effect was like a checkerboard, with the squares of tall waving grasses contained by the geometry of the smooth green paths, and the picturesque apples adding a succession of strong sculptural forms to the scene.

On large country properties here in the Northeast, I often see a vast expanse of mowed lawn stretching out beyond a house and garden, and I wonder why. Wouldn't that expanse be more beautiful, more alive, more fitting, as well as environmentally smarter, if it were waving grasses instead? If at least one path is mowed through it, the grasses and wildflowers can be enjoyed up close without any danger of attracting ticks.

The landscape architect Leslie Jones Sauer, in her excellent book *The Once and Future Forest*, recommends a method of converting a patch of lawn into a tall-grass or wildflower meadow by gradually reducing the frequency of mowing. Start with five annual mowings the first year, she says; then four the second, three the third, two the fourth, and one by the fifth year. For that once-a-year cut, she suggests not mowing until at least two hard frosts, so that all the species have had a chance to set seed. I'm going to try this five-year reduction of mowing in our mini-meadow underneath the apple trees.

Meadows, I've learned, are not maintenance-free. But they are far less taxing on us and on our land than lawn.

WATER AT THE READY

A simple but worthy enhancement of the garden on which Bosco insisted after settling at Duck Hill was easily available water. Not in the form of an automatic watering system, spewing out rain whether a plant needs it or not, nor unsightly black rubber soaker hoses snaking through the beds. No, what he introduced was a bunch of old-fashioned spigots. He called the plumber and had trenches dug one foot deep, and plastic water lines sunk throughout the garden, running up copper pipes to spigots attached to wooden posts. The posts, about three feet high, were tucked discreetly behind hedges in the various garden rooms, or among ferns at strategic points along the woodland path. Beneath each of these spigots in spring and summer, a tin watering can waits to be filled and carried to a newly planted flower or shrub. Hoses are coiled nearby, out of sight, to give parched plants a longer drink in a droughty summer. Before winter frost grips the land, the pipes are drained and blown out, the spigots left open until the following spring.

All those years before Bosco, I lugged buckets from the house, or dragged long lengths of hose from there to the gardens, cursing as the striped coils kinked, blocking the flow of water, or flattened plants as I pulled them around a bed's corner. I've always believed that an established garden should not require much watering, that it should be so well planted and suitable to its place that it doesn't need additional irrigation. But newly planted subjects need coddling at first. It is better to

At the spigot

water deeply, say once a week, than to water lightly more often. If rain does not oblige, shrubs and trees require generous drinks once a week for the first year after planting; in very dry weather, trees, even in their second or third year, will benefit from an occasional hour of watering from a slow-dribbling hose. Baby perennials need to be watched, and shallow-rooted vegetables, as well as potted plants, will not flourish without a regular dousing. As for lawns, they're on their own as far as I'm concerned, and if they turn brown and crackling in a drought, so be it. I know with autumn rains they will green up again.

Why not have an irrigation system in the garden? you ask. Because one plant might need watering while the adjacent plant does not, and an automatic system doesn't discriminate. Garden designers tear their hair out at the rotting that happens in clients' flower borders where sprinkler systems kick in for thirty minutes a day, whether it is raining or not. I want to have the luxury to choose which plants I water, based on their individual needs. So, instead of lifting weights at a gym, we lift our brimming-full watering cans, guts sucked in, to dispense irrigation on the worthy few.

We are, however, considering a more general watering system in one place—our naturally dry woodland. The esteemed gardener Frank Cabot, visiting Duck Hill once, suggested running copper water lines five or six feet up the trunks of some of our woodland trees, then attaching sprinkler nozzles to the end of those pencil-thin pipes. These could be turned on occasionally when we are deprived of rain. Unlike the denizens of the flower borders, I cannot think of a plant in our wooded patch of garden—primrose, fern, lungwort, heuchera, azalea, kirengeshoma, disanthus, hydrangea—that would not benefit from an added shower now and then in the heat of summer.

We cannot water too much at Duck Hill, because we depend on our own well, and we worry about it running dry. After much more than an hour with the sprinkler on, our water pressure indoors is reduced to a trickle. It is providential that we are forced not to overuse this precious resource. But when a plant really needs a drink, the spigots are conveniently at hand.

ADAPTING, SHRINKING, SIMPLIFYING

Gardens are supposed to get shadier as they get older. Trees grow up, hedges loom, shrubs widen and crowd against one another like passengers on a subway. But lately our garden is getting sunnier. The white ash trees on our property, as elsewhere in our neighborhood, are dying yearly, succumbing to a fungus for which there is no cure. One old fellow thrust his graceless limbs skyward near the swimming pool, shedding his leaves with the first hint of fall, and I am glad to have him gone. Another, in decline, stands sentinel by our barn, appropriate in his plain sturdiness to that structure, and will be mourned when finally we are forced to chop him down. Most of the ashes, however, thread through our small woodland, and, now with their gradual demise, a welcome light streams through the remaining maples and locusts, where we formerly struggled with deep shade.

The sudden loss of some of our great maples is not so welcome. Three years ago, a mini-tornado swept through and, within a minute, toppled three of the sugar maples that towered over our southern boundary. Two other giants lost half their trunks and died this summer. These maples formed the background of the hedged-in gardens below the house, and provided a perfect high, dappled shade to the beginning of the woodland garden. Without warning, our hostas, ferns, trilliums, and primulas were exposed, burning beneath a blazing sun. We covered them with baskets and spread newspapers over their wilted leaves while we debated what to do, and finally decided to plant a half dozen small dogwood trees to provide a quickly realized shade for this woodland understory. The following spring, we planted an eight-foot red oak at the property line, envisioning its stature long after we are gone. Several other oak seedlings, rooted in the humusy ground from acorns dropped by hoarding squirrels, responding to the new light, are shooting up rapidly in the emptied sky.

Adapting to sudden death is part of the natural cycle of gardening, never as tragic as it is in life, for we can immediately immerse ourselves in acts of renewal, in the inevitable resurgence of plants. I miss those great old trees sheltering our garden, but at the same time I am excited to see the youthful dogwoods start to spread their lovely limbs. The growth of the stripling oaks is thrilling to observe, not as slow as it is said to be, sometimes a foot a year. The gardens below the house will change with the added sunlight, and some of the shade lovers will have to be moved. But perhaps the privet hedge along that southern border, listing at a forty-five-degree angle into the garden beds away from the shade of those great trees, will now stand up straight, and the rugosa roses and hydrangeas adjacent to it will flower with more abandon.

It is not just sudden sunshine or crowding overgrowth in the garden that requires us to adapt. It is our own diminishing capabilities. I worry as we get older (Bosco is seventy-six this year and I am seventy) how we will cope with this labor-intensive creation of mine, and I know the answer is to simplify, to shrink, to cut down radically on its maintenance. Still blessed with good health and fired with enthusiasm, we're not quite ready to do this on a grand scale. We don't intend to sweep away our hedged rooms of gardens with their punctuations of boxwood. But we can gradually replace the flowers within their confines with shrubs, as Courtney did in Virginia. We've begun this process in the hemlock garden as well as in the main garden.

I've been unhappy with the look of the hemlock garden for years, wishing I hadn't dug those double borders in the first place. With aging, the garden became lopsided, the roses and perennials thriving at one end and languishing at the other, and the continuity of the borders was lost. Eventually, I might do away with the flower beds altogether, merely leaving a green alley between the two hedges. But for now, I wanted to try a planting that was dramatic in its simplicity, filling the beds with masses of one shrub that would be appealing in every season.

Last September we pulled out the great old roses that still thrived, the lavish 'Sarah Van Fleet' and rose-pink 'Thérèse Bugnet', heartbreaking to do as they proffered a few precious autumn blooms. Originally grafted and too old and woody to save, we hauled them to a branch pile for chipping. Perennials were moved or discarded, and the beds were turned over with wheelbarrows of compost. We left the boxwood bushes in place, and added a low edging of box along the front of the borders. This spring, we planted the long double beds with one shrub, a dwarf form of the variegated red-twigged dogwood, *Cornus alba* 'Bailhalo'. It ought to fare well in the half-shaded beds, and its white-edged foliage should light up this shadowy place throughout spring and summer. In winter its crimson twigs will color the garden.

We then planted ground covers to help suppress weeds. Pink and rose varieties of cranesbills that had been in the garden were divided and replanted throughout the beds. Around them we wove the Japanese tassel fern, *Polystichum polyblepharum*, its bouquets of glossy, crinkled evergreen leaves a rich contrast. Not able to leave well enough alone, we added white double Japanese anemones for some tall, swaying flowers among the dogwood branches in fall. This October we will tuck in drifts of the April-flowering cyclamineus daffodil 'Jenny', with narrow ivory trumpet and flared-back petals, and the June-blooming Sicilian honey garlic, *Nectaroscordum siculum*, its tall dangling bells of white flushed with carmine and green. Nevertheless, flowers are merely incidental here now; the overall effect is of a continuous pattern and texture of leaves, and, in winter, of reddened stems. The hemlock garden should require less work. As the small shrubs expand and knit together, the anemones will be pushed out, and all that will remain around them are ground covers and the bulbs. I hope it will present a handsome if quiet picture.

It is hard to garden with restraint. We have so many ideas; we want to collect and grow so many plants. Sometimes, when pockets are full, we are in danger of going too far in our plans, in overdoing our gardens with an excess of design and planting, losing any clarity of purpose or vision. We've all walked

Sicilian honey garlic

through overly ambitious gardens that just don't seem to end, where, after a while, we just want to go away to somewhere quiet. As we grow older, it becomes easier to admire simplicity, even to long for it. A sweep of one plant often moves me more now than the razzle-dazzle of brilliant mixtures of color and patterns. Drifts of blue phlox through a wood. Pools of camassia by a stream. A carpet of daffodils. A field of switchgrass rustling in the least breeze. In simplifying our design and our palette, we achieve a welcome serenity.

I went to a friend's garden in the hills north of here recently and fell in love. A long drive curved past an orchard of standard apple trees on one side and a wood-edged field on the other, ending at an eighteenth-century farmhouse and barn sheltered beneath great old maples and oaks. Everywhere, all around the house, were meadows, soft, waving plains of grass and native flowers, with generous paths mowed through them. A vegetable garden was discreetly fenced to one side, half hidden by wild blueberry bushes. The house embraced a stone terrace where a wood arbor woven with Concord grapes cast a welcome shade. Off to one side of the property, a boardwalk snaked through wetland, where clethra and winterberry and red maples flourished. That was all. Some would say it wasn't really a garden, except for the vegetable plot; just a landscape. But this land was planted and nurtured, views cut, paths mowed, the trees cared for, the apples pruned. Even though the only flowers were goldenrod in the meadow and apple blossoms in the orchard and racemes of fragrant clethra in the marshland, it was surely a garden: one, I thought, of serene beauty.

I was struck that day with a longing for that simpler, quieter place, ready to give up my flowers, turn my back on Duck Hill, the busyness of its confined rooms, the sense of always being on the edge of chaos with constant tending needed. My reaction to my friend's garden left me stunned, for until that moment the thought of ever leaving here seemed unbearable.

It was a healthy revelation. I worry less now, feel more at ease. If the day comes when we are no longer able to keep this garden maintained, when we have simplified it as much as we dare and it is still beyond our physical capacities and our purse strings, somewhere a meadow and orchard will beckon and make it easier to leave Duck Hill.

FINAL THREADS

PERFECTION

Years of visiting gardens around America and much of Europe have shaped and colored my thoughts on what makes a garden special. What sort of garden appeals to me most? The style of it doesn't seem to matter, as long as it reflects its surroundings, nor whether it's grand or modest. What stirs and excites me in a garden is a certain atmosphere, a mood, romantic perhaps, or fiercely wild (that garden of writhing cactuses and succulents at the Huntington Library) or sublimely serene, such as a garden of green mosses, rocks, and ferns beneath silvery beech trees. I thrill to evidence of a passion, a clarity of purpose, imagination, and humor.

Sometimes I see a perfectly ordered garden that seems dull to me because it lacks either mood, imagination, or humor. When all the flowers are standing up straight, the hedges exactly squared, the edges trimmed, the topiaries uniformly round, when there's not a weed in sight or a plant out of place and there's nothing unexpected, a garden in all its tidiness can seem without soul. Where are nature's touches, the serendipitous accidents that make a garden charming? Where is the vision, the sense of fun? Better for the gardener to relax a bit, let go, loosen his or her imagination, play with new and different ideas, whatever their outcome. Of course, a certain precision is expected in a formal garden; but one beautiful tree off-center, one stray flower at the edge of a path, one wayward branch weeping over a hedge, give that garden an unexpected grace.

At Duck Hill there is no risk of achieving perfection. We are never in full control of what goes on in the garden, never without the sometimes fortuitous surprises that come of neglect, of not weeding well enough, not mulching heavily. "Many things go undone," Louise Beebe Wilder wrote about her own garden, "and while this in one sense is a trial, in another we gain, for with more meticulous care many valuable seedlings would be housemaided out of existence and we should be immeasurably poorer."

"It must be beautiful," a client of mine once demanded through gritted teeth when I agreed to design her garden. She only cared what others would see. And I thought silently, No, it must be beautiful to *you*; a garden should be your own private joy, your own delight, no matter what others think. Perfection is captured in a leaf, in an unfurling flower or a ripened fruit—that is enough. Our gardens are imperfect, ever-changing works of art, but, in the best of worlds, they are the results of a passion, our joyous individual efforts of expression in color, pattern, and texture, woven with leaves and flowers, in partnership with nature.

REFUGE

The garden is a constant in my ever-changing life. Yes, the garden changes too, but being in it, absorbed by it, loving it, does not alter. Here, the cares of life, the tensions and headaches, evaporate as I sink deeply, satisfyingly into *its* cares, its development. It is like a child, nurtured, loved, criticized, fussed over, a possessive attachment, wrenching to leave, even for a short vacation. Like a child, it is only barely controlled, always offering surprises, unexpected nuances. I feel a quiet joy in its awakening, at its unexpected beauty, distress as weeds encroach on its verges and beetles and caterpillars ravage it, responsibility, even guilt, when sickness and death visit it. The garden figuratively as well as literally brings me down to earth. I care nothing for material pleasures when I am lost in its workings, absorbed in its embroidery. I am at peace, content.

Life at Duck Hill has not always been blissful. I've struggled through times of anguish and upheaval. The garden was my refuge, my sanctuary, a place of solace. It remains this today, though I share it gladly with Bosco, our haven in a world of turmoil, our escape from the frenzied pace we can easily slip into, rushing from appointment to appointment, with barely a moment spared to stop and look around us. Gardens "have a way of slowing time down—allowing its flow to gather in placid ponds, as it were—but that is part of their power of enchantment," Robert Pogue Harrison writes

Duck Hill

in his thoughtful book *Gardens*. They are not memorials, he says, "they do not exist to immortalize their makers or defy the ravages of time. If anything, they exist to reenchant the present."